ENGLISH GRAMMAR FOR STUDENTS OF SPANISH

The Study Guide for Those Learning Spanish

Second Edition

By
Emily Spinelli
The University of Michigan, Dearborn

The Olivia and Hill Press®

English Grammar series
  edited by Jacqueline Morton

English Grammar for Students of French, 2nd edition
English Grammar for Students of Spanish, 2nd edition
English Grammar for Students of German, 2nd edition
English Grammar for Students of Italian
English Grammar for Students of Latin
English Grammar for Students of Russian

Printed in the U.S.A.

Library of Congress Catalog Card Number: 79-90976

ISBN 0-934034-13-3

10 9 8 7 6

Contents

To the Student

English Grammar for Students of Spanish is a handbook that will help you get the most out of your Spanish textbook as well as answer some of the questions you might be reluctant to ask in class.

Most teachers incorporate **English Grammar** into the class syllabus so you will know which pages to read before doing an assignment in your Spanish textbook. If you have to select the pages yourself, check the index to find where the grammatical terms and concepts you will be studying in the textbook are covered in this handbook.

How to Use the English Grammar Handbook

- Read carefully, making sure you understand the explanations and the examples.
- Do the **Practice** at the end of the chapter you have read.
- Compare your answers with the Answer Key at the end of the handbook. If they don't match, review the section.

Now you are ready to do your assignment in your textbook.

Tips for Studying a Foreign Language

It is generally accepted that the two most important elements in learning a foreign language are vocabulary and grammar. Words (vocabulary) and the way in which they are formed and combined (grammar) together make up the ideas or messages that people wish to communicate. As a student you must learn the vocabulary and grammar presented in the classroom and textbook. This will in turn allow you to develop the four skill areas of language: listening, speaking, reading, and writing.

The following suggestions will help you improve your ability to learn the vocabulary and grammar and to become a successful foreign language learner.

1. **Practice in sequence**—Your Spanish textbook presents material in a sequential fashion; that is, each chapter and section of each chapter present new material that depends upon previously learned material. You need to learn the material in the order that it is presented; make sure you understand each section before moving on to the next one. Remember that language learning is like building a house; each brick is only as secure as its foundation.

2. **Daily practice**—Set aside a block of time each day for studying Spanish. Don't get behind. It's almost impossible to catch up because you need time to absorb the material and to develop the skills.

3. **Active practice**—Practice the textbook exercises out loud; silent reading will not develop your speaking skill. Follow your speaking practice with the written exercises of the workbook. In this way the writing reinforces your speaking and vice versa. It also helps you learn vocabulary and grammar forms.

4. **Listening practice**—Listen to the audio tapes in the school language laboratory or on your own tape player. Listen for short periods of time several times per week. Four fifteen minute sessions over four days are far more beneficial than one hour-long session.

5. **Memorization**—Memorization plays an important part in language learning. For instance, you will have to memorize vocabulary, verb conjugations, and grammar rules. Learning vocabulary and verb endings in the context of complete sentences is easier and more efficient than learning them in isolation. As you do the exercises in the textbook, you will begin to learn the vocabulary and grammar. After doing the exercises and before exams, use the vocabulary lists and verb charts of the textbook to check if you really do know the material.

6. **Vocabulary**—In addition to the suggestions given under Memorization, here are some other means to learn vocabulary that students have found useful.

Write each word on a separate index card, Spanish on one side, English on the other.

Use index cards or pens of different colors. This can help you remember other useful information about the word: using blue for masculine nouns and pink for feminine nouns will help you remember genders. (You can also use green for verbs, orange for adjectives, etc. to remember parts of speech.)

When learning the Spanish words, look at the English words. Say aloud the Spanish word that corresponds; then flip the card to check your answer. Shuffle the deck often so you see the English word cold (i.e., without remembering the word order).

7. **Proficiency**—The principle goal of your Spanish instruction is for you to be able to communicate with Spanish speakers and to function in a Spanish-speaking country. Learning vocabulary and grammar is not the end goal; it is a means to develop your proficiency in listening, speaking, reading, and writing. Keeping the goal in mind will help you see the purpose behind the exercises you do and will ultimately help make you a successful language learner.

Buena suerte,
Emily Spinelli

Introduction

When you learn a foreign language, in this case Spanish, you must look at each word in three ways.

1. **Meaning** of a word. Each English word must be connected to a Spanish word that has an equivalent meaning.

    The English word *book* has the same meaning as the Spanish word **libro**.

    Words with equivalent meanings are learned by memorizing **vocabulary** items. Sometimes two words are the same or very similar in both English and Spanish. These words are called **cognates** and are, of course, easy to learn.

SPANISH	ENGLISH
inteligente	intelligent
problema	problem
visitar	visit

Occasionally knowing one Spanish word will help you learn another.

    Knowing that **niño** means *boy* should help you learn that **niña** is *girl*; or knowing that **hermano** is *brother* should help you remember that **hermana** is *sister*.

Usually, however, there is little similarity between words and knowing one Spanish word will not help you learn another. As a general rule, you must memorize each vocabulary item separately.

    Knowing that *man* is **hombre** will not help you learn that *woman* is **mujer**.

In addition, there are times when words in combination take on a special meaning.

The Spanish word **hacer** means *to make*; **cola** means *tail*. However, **hacer cola** means *to line up, to stand in line*.

Such an expression whose meaning as a whole (**hacer cola**) is different from the meaning of the individual words (**hacer** and **cola**) is called and **idiom**. You will need to pay special attention to those idiomatic expressions in order to recognize them and use them correctly.

2. **Classification** of a word. English and Spanish words are classified into eight categories called **parts of speech**. Here is a list of the parts of speech used in Spanish.

noun	article
verb	adverb
pronoun	preposition
adjective	conjunction

Each part of speech has its own rules for spelling, pronunciation and use. You must learn to recognize what part of speech a word is in order to choose the correct Spanish equivalent and know what rules to apply. Look at the word *that* in the following sentences.

   a. *That* girl is my sister.
   b. There is the car *that* he bought.
   c. We didn't talk about *that*.

The English word is the same in all three sentences, but in Spanish three different words will be used because each *that* belongs to a different part of speech.[1]

---

[1] a. Demonstrative adjective, see p. 151.
  b. Relative pronoun, see p. 227.
  c. Demonstrative pronoun, see p. 212.

3. **Use** of a word. Each word, whether English or Spanish, plays a specific role in a sentence. Identifying or determining this role or **function** will help you choose the correct Spanish equivalent and know which rules to apply.

Let us examine the function of the word *him* in the following sentences.

    a. They don't see *him*.
    b. I wrote *him* a letter.
    c. Are you going with *him*?

Because the word *him* has a different function in each sentence above, its Spanish equivalent will be different in each sentence.[1]

As a student of Spanish you must learn to recognize both the parts of speech and the function of each word in a sentence.

This is essential because words in a Spanish sentence have a great deal of influence on one another.

*The new red **shoes** are on the small round table.*

Los nuevos **zapatos** rojos están sobre la pequeña **mesa** redonda.

In English: The only word that affects another word in the sentence is *shoes*, which forces us to use *are*. If the word were *shoe*, we would have to use *is*.

---

[1] a. Direct Object, see p. 184.
   b. Indirect Object, see p. 184.
   c. Object of a preposition, see p. 190.

In Spanish: The word for *shoes* (**zapatos**) not only affects the word for *are* (**están**), but also the spelling and pronunciation of the Spanish words for *the, new,* and *red.* The word for table (**mesa**) affects the spelling and pronunciation of the Spanish words *the, small,* and *round.* The only word not affected by another word is **sobre,** meaning *on.*

Since parts of speech and function are usually determined in the same way in English and in Spanish, this handbook will show you how to identify them in English. You will then learn to compare English and Spanish constructions. This will give you a better understanding of the grammar explanations in your Spanish textbook.

What is a Noun?

A **noun** is a word that can be the name of a person, animal, place, thing, event, or idea.

In English: Let us look at some different types of words that are nouns.

a person	professor, clown, student, girl, baby, Dr. Smith, Bill, Mary
an animal	elephant, horse, snake, eagle, Lassie, Bambi, Garfield, Teddy
a place	city, state, country, continent, Madrid, Michigan, Mexico, South America
a thing	apple, lamp, dress, airplane, the White House, a Cadillac
an event or activity	graduation, shopping, marriage, skiing, birth, the Olympics, Thanksgiving
an idea or concept	democracy, humor, hatred, elegance, time, love, justice, poverty

As you can see, a noun can be a word that names something tangible, that is, something you can touch, such as a *lamp, horse,* or *Cadillac.* Or, a noun can also be a word that names something abstract or intangible that you cannot touch, such as *love, justice,* or *graduation.*

A noun that does not state the name of specific person, place, or thing, etc. is called a **common noun**. A common noun does not begin with a capital letter, unless it is the first word of a sentence. All the nouns in the preceding list that are not capitalized are common nouns.

A noun that is the name of a specific person, place, thing, etc. is called a **proper noun**. A proper noun always begins with a capital letter. All the nouns in the preceding list that are capitalized are proper nouns.

Bill Smith is my best friend.

proper   common
nouns   noun

A noun that is made up of two or more words is called a **compound noun**. A compound noun can be a common noun such as *ice cream* or *comic strip*, or a proper noun, such as *South America* or *Mexico City*.

To help you learn to recognize nouns, look at the paragraph below where the nouns are in ***bold type***.

The ***countries*** that make up the Spanish-speaking ***world*** export ***products*** that we use every ***day***. ***Spain*** produces many of the ***shoes, purses***, and ***gloves*** that are sold in ***stores*** throughout the ***United States***. ***Spain*** also sells us much ***wine, sherry***, and ***brandy***. The ***islands*** of the ***Caribbean*** and the ***nations*** of ***Central America*** supply us with tropical ***fruits*** such as ***bananas*** and ***melons***; ***sugar*** is another important ***export*** of these ***regions***. While ***oil*** is a major ***source*** of ***income*** for ***Mexico*** and ***Venezuela***, the ***economies*** of several other ***countries*** of ***Latin America*** depend upon the ***production*** and ***exportation*** of ***coffee***.

In Spanish: Nouns are identified in the same way they are in English.

<small>TERMS USED TO TALK ABOUT NOUNS</small>

- A noun has gender, that is, it can be classified according to whether it is masculine, feminine, or neuter (see **What is Meant by Gender?**, p. 7).

- A noun has number; that is, it can be identified according to whether it is singular or plural (see **What is Meant by Number?**, p. 12).

- A noun can have a variety of functions in a sentence; that is, it can be the subject of the sentence (see **What is a Subject?**, p. 32 or an object (see **What are Objects?**, p. 173).

Practice

Circle the nouns in the following sentences.

1. The student came into the classroom and spoke to the teacher.

2. The Wilsons went on a tour of Mexico.

3. Honesty is the best policy.

4. Lisa wants a new carpet for her bedroom.

5. Figure skating is always an exciting event in the Winter Olympics.

6. Scientists are afraid that elephants will become extinct.

7. I pledge allegiance to the flag of the United States of America.

8. Buenos Aires, the capital of Argentina, is a very cosmopolitan city.

9. Truth is stranger than fiction.

10. Monday is the worst day of the week.

11. They want a manager with intelligence and a sense of humor.

What is Meant by Gender?

When a word can be classified as masculine, feminine, or neuter, it is said to have **gender.**

Gender is not very important in English. However, it is at the very heart of the Spanish language because the gender of a word often affects the way a word is spelled and pronounced. More parts of speech have gender in Spanish than in English as the list indicates.

ENGLISH	SPANISH
pronouns	nouns
possessive adjectives	pronouns
	articles
	adjectives

Each part of speech follows its own rules to indicate gender. In this section we will look only at the gender of nouns. You will find the rules for gender of articles and the various types of pronouns and adjectives in the sections dealing specifically with those items.

In English: Nouns themselves do not have a gender, but sometimes their meaning will indicate a gender based on the biological sex of the person or animal named by the noun. When we replace a proper or common noun with *he* or *she,* we automatically use *he* for males and *she* for females. All the nouns that name things that do not have a sex are replaced by *it.*

Nouns referring to males indicate the **masculine** gender.

> Paul came home; *he* was tired, and I was glad to see *him.*
> noun   masculine   masculine
> male

Nouns referring to females indicate the **feminine** gender.

> The girl came home; *she* was tired and I was glad to see *her.*
> noun   feminine   feminine
> female

All other nouns do not indicate a gender; they are considered
neuter.[1]

The city of Washington is lovely. I enjoyed visiting *it*.
    |
   noun   neuter

In Spanish: All nouns–common nouns and proper nouns–are either
masculine or feminine. There is no such thing as a noun without
gender or a neuter gender.

The **biological gender** is the gender of nouns whose meaning is
always tied to one or the other of the biological sexes, male or
female. The gender of these nouns is easy to determine.

MALES = MASCULINE	FEMALES = FEMININE
Paul	Mary
boy	girl
brother	sister
stepfather	niece

You must make sure, however, that the noun can refer to only one
sex or the other. For instance, "father" can only be a male; therefore, the Spanish noun for "father" is of the masculine gender. The
noun "student," however, can refer to a male or a female. Therefore
the meaning of the noun itself will not reveal its gender.

The gender of all other nouns, common and proper, cannot be
explained or figured out. These nouns have a **grammatical gender**
that is unrelated to biological gender.

---

[1] There are a few well-known exceptions, such as *ship*, which is referred to as *she*. It is custom,
not logic, that decides.

The S/S United States sailed for Europe. *She* was a beautiful ship.

SOME ENGLISH NOUNS WITH *MASCULINE* EQUIVALENTS IN SPANISH	SOME ENGLISH NOUNS WITH *FEMININE* EQUIVALENTS IN SPANISH
money	coin
book	library
country	nation
Peru	Argentina
heaven	war
Wednesday	peace
sorrow	health
problem	philosophy

You will need to know the gender of every Spanish noun you learn. This gender is important not only for the noun itself, but for the spelling of the words it influences.

ENDINGS INDICATING GENDER

Gender can sometimes be determined by looking at the end of the Spanish noun. In the lists that follow there are endings that often indicate feminine nouns and others that indicate masculine nouns. Since you will encounter many nouns with these endings in basic Spanish, it is certainly worthwhile to familiarize yourself with them.[1]

	FEMININE ENDINGS	
-a	la casa, la biblioteca	*house, library*
-dad, -tad	la ciudad, la libertad	*city, liberty*
-z	la nariz	*nose*
-ión, -ción	la reunión, la nación	*meeting, nation*
-umbre	la costumbre	*custom*
-ie	la especie	*species*

---

[1] This table of endings has been adapted from John J. Bergen. "A Simplified Approach for Teaching the Gender of Spanish Nouns." *Hispania*, LXI (December, 1978), 875.

MASCULINE ENDINGS

Any ending except those provided in the Feminine Endings list. In particular:

-l	el papel	*paper*
-o	el libro	*book*
-n	el jardín	*garden*
-e	el parque	*park*
-r	el dolor	*pain*
-s	el interés	*interest*

To help you remember these endings note that for the masculine endings the letters spell "loners."

There are of course many exceptions to the above rules: **la mano** (*hand*) and **el día** (*day*) are two common exceptions. Your textbook and instructor will point out the exceptions that you will need to learn.

Practice

A. The Spanish gender of some English nouns is obvious; for others you will need to consult a dictionary. Read the list below. Write *masculine* or *feminine* next to the nouns whose gender you can identify. Write "*?*" next to the nouns whose gender you would have to look up.

GENDER IN SPANISH

1. boys   *masculine*

2. chair   *masculine*

3. wife   *feminine*

4. uncles   *masculine*

5. dress ~~masculine~~ *masculine*

6. motorcycle *masculine*

7. grandmother *feminine*

8. house *feminine*

B. Write the word *masculine* or *feminine* next to the following nouns. Use the lists for feminine and masculine endings on pp. 9–10 to help you identify gender.

GENDER

1. postre *masculine*

2. universidad *feminine*

3. chica *feminine*

4. amor *masculine*

5. hotel *masculine*

6. cuarto *masculine*

7. televisión *feminine*

8. examen *masculine*

What is Meant by Number?

When a word refers to one person or thing, it is said to be **singular**; when it refers to more than one, it is **plural**.

More parts of speech indicate number in Spanish than in English; there are also more spelling and pronunciation changes in Spanish as the following list indicates.

ENGLISH	SPANISH
nouns	nouns
verbs	verbs
pronouns	pronouns
only demonstrative	adjectives
adjectives	articles

Each part of speech follows its own rules to indicate number. In this section we will look only at the number of nouns. You will find the rule for number of articles and various types of pronouns and adjectives in the sections dealing specifically with those items.

In English: A singular noun is made plural in two basic ways:

- by adding **-s** or **-es** to the end of the singular noun

book	books
church	churches

- by making a spelling change

man	men
mouse	mice
leaf	leaves
child	children

A plural noun is generally spelled and pronounced differently from the singular.

Some nouns, called **collective nouns**, refer to a group of persons or things, but the noun itself is considered singular.

> A football *team* has eleven players.
> My *family* is well.
> The *crowd* was under control.

In Spanish: As in English, the plural form of a noun is usually spelled differently from the singular. There are two basic ways to form a plural noun.

- Nouns that end in a vowel add **-s** to form a plural:

casa	casas	*house*	*houses*
libro	libros	*book*	*books*

- Nouns that end in a consonant add **-es** to form a plural:

papel	papeles	*paper*	*papers*
ciudad	ciudades	*city*	*cities*

A few nouns will have internal spelling changes when they become plural. One such common change is **-z** to **-c-**: lápiz ⟶ lápices (*pencil* ⟶ *pencils*). Your textbook will point out other exceptions to the two basic rules listed above.

NOTE: Nouns do not change gender when they become plural.

Practice:

A. Look at the following English words. Circle (s) if the word is
singular and (P) if the word is plural.

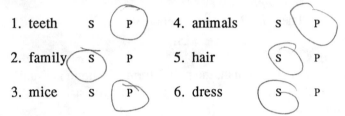

    1. teeth   s (P)   4. animals   s (P)

    2. family (s) P   5. hair   (s) P

    3. mice   s (P)   6. dress (s) P

B. Look at the following Spanish words. Make the words plural by
circling (-s) or (-ES) according to the rules.

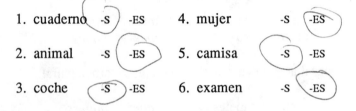

    1. cuaderno (-S) -ES   4. mujer   -S (-ES)

    2. animal   -S (-ES)   5. camisa (-S) -ES

    3. coche (-S) -ES   6. examen -S (-ES)

What are Articles?

An **article** is a word placed before a noun to show whether the noun
refers to a particular person, animal, place, thing, event, or idea, or
whether the noun refers to an unspecified person, thing, or idea.

In English: Let us look at the two types of articles.

    1. A **definite article** is used before a noun when we are speaking
    about a particular person, place, animal, thing, or idea. There is
    one definite article: ***the***.

        I saw *the* boy you spoke to me about.
           |
          a particular boy

        I ate *the* apple you gave me.
           |
          a particular apple

The definite article remains *the* when the noun that follows becomes plural.

> I saw *the* boys you spoke to me about.
> I ate *the* apples you gave me.

2. An **indefinite article** is used before a noun when we are speaking about an unspecified person, animal, place, thing, event, or idea. There are two indefinite articles: **a** and **an**.

> *A* is used before a word beginning with a consonant.[1]

> I saw *a* boy in the street.

> *An* is used before a word beginning with a vowel.

> I ate *an* apple.

The indefinite articles *a/an* are used only with singular nouns; they are dropped when the noun becomes plural. At times the word *some* is used as a replacement.

> I saw boys in the street.
> I saw *some* boys in the street.
> I ate apples.
> I ate *some* apples.

In Spanish: You will have to pay much more attention to Spanish definite and indefinite articles than you do to their English equivalents. In Spanish the article works hand in hand with the noun it belongs to and matches the noun's gender and number. This "matching" is called **agreement**. Your textbook and instructor will

---

[1] Vowels are the sounds associated with the letters *a, e, i, o, u* and sometimes *y*; consonants are the sounds associated with the other letters of the alphabet.

say that "the article must agree with the noun in gender and number." This means that a different article is used depending on whether the noun is masculine or feminine, and depending on whether the noun is singular or plural. Because these articles are both pronounced and spelled differently, they indicate the gender and number of the noun to the ear as well as to the eye.

1. There are four forms of the definite article.

El indicates a masculine singular noun.

el libro	*the book*
el muchacho	*the boy*

La indicates a feminine singular noun.

la casa	*the house*
la muchacha	*the girl*

Los indicates a masculine plural noun.

los libros	*the books*
los muchachos	*the boys*

Las indicates a feminine plural noun.

las casas	*the houses*
las muchachas	*the girls*

The definite article is used much more frequently in Spanish than in English.

La química es difícil.
Chemistry is difficult.

Esa mujer es **la** señora Gómez.
That lady is Mrs. Gómez.

Memorize nouns with the singular definite article; in most cases the article will tell you if the noun is masculine or feminine.[1]

2. There are four forms of the indefinite article.

Un indicates a masculine singular noun.

> **un** libro   *a book*
> **un** muchacho   *a boy*

Una indicates a feminine singular noun.

> **una** casa   *a house*
> **una** muchacha   *a girl*

Unos indicates a masculine plural noun.

> **unos** libros   *some books*
> **unos** muchachos   *some boys*

Unas indicates a feminine plural noun.

> **unas** casas   *some houses*
> **unas** muchachas   *some girls*

Your textbook will instruct you on additional uses of the definite and indefinite articles in Spanish.

---

[1]There are only a few exceptions to this statement. The primary exceptions are those feminine nouns that begin with a stressed **a-** and which for pronunciation purposes take **el** as the article: **el agua, el águila**. The noun is nonetheless still feminine: el agua **fría**.

Practice

A. Each of the following English words is preceded by an article. Circle (D) for definite or (I) for indefinite depending if the noun is accompanied by a definite or an indefinite article.

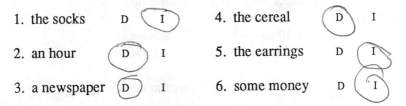

1. the socks   D (I)   4. the cereal   (D) I

2. an hour   (D) I   5. the earrings   D (I)

3. a newspaper (D) I   6. some money   D (I)

B. The following list contains some singular and some plural nouns in English. The DICTIONARY ENTRY gives you the Spanish noun and shows you if that noun (n.) is masculine (m.) or feminine (f.).
  • Write the appropriate form of the Spanish definite article and noun in the space provided.

DICTIONARY ENTRY		SPANISH DEFINITE ARTICLE PLUS NOUN
1. books	libro (*n.m.*)	los libro
2. table	mesa (*n.f.*)	the mesa
3. classes	clase (*n.f.*)	~~la clase~~ ane clase
4. telephone	teléfono (*n.m.*)	el teléfono
5. cars	coche (*n.m.*)	~~los~~ coche
6. sister	hermana (*n.f.*)	la hermana

C. Write the appropriate form of the Spanish indefinite article for the nouns in Exercise B.

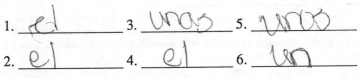

1. el   3. unas   5. unos

2. el   4. el   6. un

What is the Possessive?

The term **possessive** means that one noun owns or possesses another noun.

In English: You can show possession in one of two ways.

    1. An *apostrophe* can be used.

- an apostrophe + "s" is added to a singular possessor

      Mary's dress
        |
      singular possessor

      Picasso's paintings
      the professor's book
      a tree's branches
      the lady's purse

- an apostrophe is added to a plural possessor

      the girls' father
          |
      plural possessor

      the boys' team

    2. The word *of* can be used.

- *of* is placed before a proper noun possessor.

      the dress *of* Mary
               |
      proper noun possessor

      the paintings *of* Picasso

- *of the* or *of a* is placed before a singular or plural common noun possessor.

     the book *of the* professor
                              |
     singular common noun possessor

     the branches *of a* tree
     the father *of the* girls
                              |
        plural common noun possessor

     the team *of the* boys

In Spanish: There is only one way to express possession and that is by using the "of" construction (2 above). The apostrophe structure does not exist. When you want to show possession in Spanish, you must change an English structure using an apostrophe to a structure using *of* (**de**).

Mary's dress	*the dress of Mary* el vestido **de** María
the professor's book	*the book of the professor* el libro **del** profesor

                                              el libro **del** profesor
                                                              |
                                           ┌──────────────┐
                                           │   de + el   │
                                           └──────────────┘

the lady's purse	*the purse of the lady* la bolsa **de la** señora
a tree's branches	*the branches of a tree* las ramas **de un** árbol
the girls' father	*the father of the girls* el padre **de las** muchachas
the boys' team	*the team of the boys* el equipo **de los** muchachos

Practice:

The following are possessives using the apostrophe. Write the alternate English structure that is the word-for-word equivalent of the Spanish structure.

1. some children's parents   *Parents of some children*

2. the doctor's office   *office of the doctor*

3. a dog's life   *life of a dog*

4. the girls' soccer coach   *soccer coach of the girl*

5. Gloria Smith's mother   *mother of Gloria Smith*

What is a Verb?

A **verb** is a word that indicates "the action" of the sentence. The word "action" is used in the broadest sense, not necessarily physical action.

In English: Let us look at different types of words which are verbs.

a physical activity	to run, to hit, to talk, to walk, to wrestle
a mental activity	to hope, to believe, to imagine, to dream, to think
a condition	to be, to have, to seem

Many verbs however do not fall neatly into one of the above categories. They are verbs nevertheless because they represent the "action" of the sentence.

The book *costs* only $5.00.
|
to cost

The students *feel* tired.
|
to feel

To help you learn to recognize verbs, look at the paragraph below where the verbs are in **bold type.**

The three students **entered** the restaurant, **selected** a table, **hung** up their coats and **sat** down. They **looked** at the menu and **asked** the waitress what she **recommended.** She **advised** the daily special, beef stew. It **was** not expensive. They **chose** a bottle of red wine and **ordered** a salad. The service **was** slow, but the food **tasted** very good. Good cooking, they **decided, takes** time. They **ate** pastry for dessert and **finished** the meal with coffee.

The verb is one of the most important words in a sentence; you cannot express a complete thought (i.e., write a **complete sentence**) without a verb. It is important that you learn to identify verbs because the function of many words in a sentence often depends on their relationship to the verb. For instance, the subject of a sentence is the word doing the action of the verb, and the object is the word receiving the action of the verb (see **What is a Subject?**, p. 32 and **What are Objects?**, p. 173).

There are two types of verbs in both English and Spanish: transitive and intransitive.

1. A **transitive verb** is a verb that takes a direct object (see **What are Objects?**, p. 173). It is indicated by the abbreviation *v.t.* (*verbo transitivo*) in dictionaries.

The boy *threw* the ball.
| |
transitive   direct object

She *quit* her job.
|
transitive

2. An **intransitive verb** is a verb that does not take a direct object. It is indicated by the abbreviation *v.i.* (*verbo intransitivo*) in the dictionary.

> Paul *is sleeping.*
> |
> intransitive

> She *will arrive* soon.
> | |
> intransitive adverb

Many verbs can be used transitively or intransitively in sentences, depending on whether they have a direct object or not.

> The students *speak* Spanish.
> | |
> transitive   direct object

> Actions *speak* louder than words.
> |
> intransitive

In English it is possible to change the meaning of a verb by placing short words (prepositions or adverbs) after them. The verb *look* in Column A changes meaning depending on the word that follows it.

COLUMN A		COLUMN B
to look *for*	=	to search for
		I am looking for a book.
to look *after*	=	to take care of
		I am looking after the children.
to look *out*	=	to beware of
		Look out for the car.
to look *into*	=	to investigate
		I am looking into the problem.
to look *over*	=	to check
		I am looking over my exam.

In Spanish: Verbs are identified the same way that they are in English. However, be careful of the following two pitfalls.

1. Some verbs that are transitive in English are intransitive in Spanish, while other verbs that are intransitive in English are transitive in Spanish. Examples of these verbs are given in the section **What are Objects?**, p. 173.

2. It is impossible to change the meaning of a verb by adding short words as in Column A above. In Spanish, you would have to use an entirely different verb in each of the above sentences. When looking up verbs in the dictionary, be sure to look for the specific meaning under the dictionary entry. For instance, all the examples above under Column A will be found under the dictionary entry *look,* but you will have to search for the expression *look for* or *look after* to find the correct Spanish equivalent. Don't select the first entry under *look* and then add on the Spanish equivalent for *after*; the result will be meaningless in Spanish.

TERMS USED TO TALK ABOUT VERBS

- The verb form which is the name of the verb is called an infinitive: *to eat, to sleep, to drink* (see **What is an Infinitive?**, p. 25).

- A verb is conjugated or changes in form to agree with its subject: *I do, he does* (see **What is a Verb Conjugation?**, p. 49).

- A verb indicates tense, that is, the time (present, past, or future) of the action: *I am, I was, I will be* (see **What is Meant by Tense?**, p. 75).

- A verb shows voice, that is, the relation between the subject and the action of the verb (see **What is Meant by Active and Passive Voice?**, p. 125).

- A verb shows mood, that is the speakers' attitude toward what they are saying (see **What is Meant by Mood?**, p. 92).

- A verb may also be used to form a participle (see **What is a Participle?**, p. 84).

Practice

Circle the verbs in the following sentences.

1. The students purchase their lunch at school.

2. Paul and Mary were happy.

3. They enjoyed the movie, but they preferred the book.

4. Paul ate dinner, finished his novel, and then went to bed.

5. Mary suddenly realized that she dreamt every night.

6. The teacher felt sick yesterday, but today she seems fine.

7. The anxious parents stayed home because they expected a phone call.

8. It was sad to see the little dog struggle to get out of the lake.

9. I attended a concert to celebrate the new year.

10. The price of food increases, but my salary remains the same.

What is an Infinitive?

An **infinitive** is the name of the verb. It is under the infinitive form that you will find a verb in the dictionary.

In English: The infinitive is composed of two words *to* + the dictionary form of the verb (*to speak, to dance*). By **dictionary form**, we mean the form of the verb that is listed as the entry in the dictionary (*speak, dance*). Although the infinitive is the most basic form of the verb, it can never be used in a sentence without another verb.

To learn is exciting.

infinitive   main verb

It'*s* (it *is*) important *to be* on time.

main verb   infinitive

Paul and Mary *want to dance* together.

main verb   infinitive

It *has started to rain*.

auxiliary   infinitive

main
verb

The dictionary form of the verb, i.e., the infinitive without the *to*, is used after such verbs as *must* and *let*.

Paul *must do* his homework.

dictionary form

The parents *let* the children *see* the presents.

dictionary form

In Spanish: The infinitive form is composed of only one word that ends with the letters **-ar, -er,** or **-ir.** These letters are called the **infinitive endings.** The word *to* in the English infinitive has no Spanish equivalent.

hablar	*to speak*
comer	*to eat*
vivir	*to live*

It is important for you to remember infinitive endings so you will know which pattern to follow in conjugating that verb (see **What is a Verb Conjugation?**, p. 49).

In a sentence the infinitive form is always used for a verb that follows another verb except **ser** (*to be*), **estar** (*to be*), or **haber** (*to have*).

> *John and Mary want **to dance** together.*
> Juan y María *quieren* **bailar** juntos.
> infinitive

> *It started **to rain**.*
> *Empezó* a **llover**.
> infinitive

> *I can **leave** tomorrow.*
> *Puedo* **salir** mañana.
> infinitive

> *You should **study** more.*
> Usted *debe* **estudiar** más.
> infinitive

Notice that in the last two examples there is no "to" in the English sentence to alert you that an infinitive must be used in Spanish.

Practice

A. Dictionaries do not list all forms of a verb; you must learn to identify the dictionary form from a variety of possible verb forms so you can use the dictionary to provide the Spanish verbs you need.
   • Under what word would you look up these verbs in the dictionary?

DICTIONARY FORM

1. Paul *swam* every day last summer. _____

2. I *am* tired today. _____

3. Carol *went* to Mexico last year. _____

4. They *had* a cold.   _____

5. Ann always *does* her homework.   _____

6. I *wrote* him a letter.   _____

B. Circle the words that you would replace with an infinitive in Spanish.

1. Mary has nothing more to do today.

2. The students must study their lesson.

3. Jeff wants to learn Spanish.

4. Mary can't sing very well.

5. We hope to travel through Spain this summer.

What are Auxiliary Verbs?

A verb is called an **auxiliary verb** or **helping verb** when it helps another verb form one of its tenses (see **What is Meant by Tense?**, p. 75). When it is used alone, it functions as a main verb.

Mary *is* a girl.	*is*	MAIN VERB
Paul *has* a headache.	*has*	MAIN VERB
They *go* to the movies.	*go*	MAIN VERB
They ***have** gone* to the movies.	***have***	AUXILIARY VERB
	gone	MAIN VERB
He ***has been** gone* two weeks.	***has***	AUXILIARY VERB
	been	AUXILIARY VERB
	gone	MAIN VERB

In English: There are many auxiliary verbs, for example, *to have, to be,* and *to do.* They have two primary uses.

1. to indicate the tense of the main verb (present, past, future—see **What is Meant by Tense?**, p. 75).

Mary *is* reading a book.	PRESENT
Mary *was* reading a book.	PAST
Mary *will* read a book.	FUTURE

2. to help formulate questions

Bob *has* a dog.	*has*	MAIN VERB
Does Bob *have* a dog?	*does*	AUXILIARY VERB
	have	MAIN VERB
They *talked* on the phone.	*talked*	MAIN VERB
Did they *talk* on the phone?	*did*	AUXILIARY VERB
	talk	MAIN VERB

In Spanish: There are three verbs that can be used as auxiliary verbs: **haber** (*to have*), **estar** (*to be*), and **ser** (*to be*). The other auxiliary verbs such as *do, does, did, will,* or *would* do not exist as separate words. In Spanish their meaning is conveyed either by a different structure (see **What are Declarative and Interrogative Sentences?**, p. 64) or by the last letters of the main verb (see **What is the Past Tense?**, p. 80; **What is the Future Tense?**, p. 110; and **What is the Conditional?**, p. 114). You will find more on this topic under the different tenses.

A verb tense composed of an auxiliary verb plus a main verb is called a **compound verb**. Let us look at some examples of the compound verb tenses you will encounter in your beginning study of Spanish.

1. The auxiliary verb **haber** followed by the past participle of the main verb (see **What is a Participle?**, p. 84) is used to form the many perfect tenses (see **What are the Perfect Tenses?**, p. 104).

Present perfect tense = present tense of **haber** + past participle of main verb

El hombre **ha comido** demasiado.
auxiliary   main verb
verb

*The man **has eaten** too much.*

Past perfect tense = imperfect tense of **haber** + past particple of main verb

Los estudiantes ya **habían llegado.**
auxiliary   main verb
haber

*The students **had already arrived.***

You will learn other perfect tenses as your study of Spanish progresses.

2. The auxiliary verb **estar** followed by the present participle of the main verb (see **What is a Participle?**, p. 84) is used to form the progressive tenses. (See **What is a Progressive Tense?**, p. 89.)

Present progressive = present tense of **estar** + present participle of main verb

Estoy leyendo un libro ahora.
auxiliary   main verb
estar

I am reading a book now.

Imperfect progressive = imperfect tense of **estar** + present participle of main verb

Estábamos escuchando la radio.
     | |
auxiliary   main verb
  estar

*We **were listening** to the radio.*

You will learn other progressive tenses as you continue your Spanish studies.

3. **Ser** as an auxiliary verb is used to form the true passive voice (see **What is Meant by Active and Passive Voice?**, p. 125).

El puente **fue construido** por los romanos.
          | |
     auxiliary   main verb
        ser

*The bridge **was constructed** by the Romans.*

Practice

A. Put one line under the auxiliary verb and two under the main verb of the following English sentences.

1. Barb is talking to her mother on the phone.

2. Did you finish your homework yet?

3. I haven't seen Tom in about a week.

4. I would buy a new car but I don't have the money.

5. Does John still live in Madrid?

6. What were you doing when he called?

B. Cross out the English auxiliary verbs that are not used as auxiliaries in Spanish.

1. We will go to Peru this year.

2. What are you doing?

3. Did you write your parents this week?

4. Tom had already graduated from high school by age sixteen.

5. Do you want to go to the movies with us?

What is a Subject?

In a sentence the person or thing that performs the action is called the **subject**.[1] When you wish to find the subject of a sentence, always look for the verb first; then ask, *who?* or *what?* before the verb. The answer will be the subject.

Teresa speaks Spanish.

> *Who* speaks Spanish?
> Answer: Teresa.
> *Teresa* is the subject.
> (Note that the subject is singular. It refers to one person.)

Are the keys on the table?

> *What* is on the table?
> Answer: the keys.
> *Keys* is the subject.
> (Note that the subject is plural. It refers to more than one person.)

---

[1] The subject performs the action in an active sentence, but is acted upon in a passive sentence (see **What is Meant by Active and Passive Voice?**, p. 125).

Train yourself to ask that question to find the subject. Never assume a word is the subject because it comes first in the sentence. Subjects can be located in several different places, as you can see in the following examples (the *subject* is in boldface and *verb* is italicized):

> *Did the game start* on time?
> After playing for two hours, *Paul became* exhausted.
> Looking in the mirror *was* a little *girl.*

Some sentences have more than one main verb; you have to find the subject of each verb.

> The *boys were doing* the cooking, while *Mary was setting* the table.
>
> *Boys is the subject of were doing.*
> (Note that the subject and verb are plural.)
>
> *Mary is the subject of was setting.*
> (Note that the subject and verb are singular.)

In both English and Spanish it is important to find the subject of each verb to make sure that the subject and the verb agree; that is, you must choose the form of the verb that goes with the subject. (See **What is a Verb Conjugation?**, p. 49.)

Practice

Find the subjects in the following sentences.
- Next to Q, write the question you need to ask to find the subject.
- Next to A, write the answer to the question you just asked.

1. When the bell rang, all the children ran out.

Q: _____

A: _____

Q: _____

A: _____

2. One waiter took the order and another brought the food.

Q: _____

A: _____

Q: _____

A: _____

3. The first-year students voted for the class president.

Q: _____

A: _____

4. That assumes I am always right.

Q: _____

A: _____

Q: _____

A: _____

5. They say that Spanish is a beautiful language.

Q: _____

A: _____

Q: _____

A: _____

What is a Pronoun?

A **pronoun** is a word used in place of one or more nouns. It may stand, therefore, for a person, place, thing, event, or idea.

For instance, rather than repeating the proper noun "Paul" in the following two sentences, it is better to use a pronoun in the second sentence.

> *Paul* likes to swim. *Paul* practices every day.
> *Paul* likes to swim. *He* practices every day.

Generally a pronoun can only be used to refer to someone (or something) that has already been mentioned. The word that the pronoun replaces or refers to is called the **antecedent** of the pronoun. In the example above, the pronoun *he* refers to the proper noun *Paul*. *Paul* is the antecedent of the pronoun *he*.

In English: There are different types of pronouns, each serving a different function and following different rules. Listed below are the more important types and the sections where they are discussed in detail.

Most pronouns change in form in the different persons and according to the function they have in the sentence.

- **Subject pronouns** (see p. 37)

    I go. *They* read. *He* runs. *She* sings.

- **Direct object pronouns** (see p. 174)

    John loves *her*.
    Jane saw *him* at the theater.

- **Indirect object pronouns** (see p. 174).

  John gave *us* the book.
  My mother wrote *me* a letter.

- **Object of preposition pronouns** (p. 179).

  Robert is going to the movies with *us*.
  Don't step on *it;* walk around *it*.

- **Reflexive pronouns** — These pronouns are used with reflexive verbs to reflect the action of the verb back to the subject of the sentence (see p. 122).

  I cut *myself*. We washed *ourselves*.

- **Interrogative pronouns** — These pronouns are used in questions (see p. 201).

  Who is that? *What* do you want?

- **Demonstrative pronouns** — These pronouns are used to point out persons or things (see p. 212).

  This (one) is expensive. *That* (one) is cheap.

- **Possessive pronouns** — These pronouns are used to show possession (see p. 221).

  Whose book is that? *Mine. Yours* is on the table.

- **Relative pronouns** — These pronouns are used to introduce relative subordinate clauses (see p. 227).

  The man *who* is my instructor is very nice.
  This is the sweater *that* I bought last week.

In Spanish: Pronouns are identified in the same way as in English. The most important difference is that a pronoun agrees with the noun it replaces; that is, it must correspond in gender (and usually in number) with its antecedent.

Practice

The following sentences contain different types of pronouns.
  • Circle the pronouns.
  • Draw an arrow from the pronoun to its antecedent, or antecedents if there is more than one.

1. Did Mary call Peter? Yes, she called him last night.

2. That coat and dress are elegant but they are expensive.

3. Mary baked the cookies herself.

4. Paul and I are very tired. We went out last night.

5. If the book is not on the bed, look under it.

What is a Subject Pronoun?

A **subject pronoun** is a pronoun used as a subject of a verb.

> *He* worked while *she* read.

> Who worked? Answer: He.
> *He* is the subject of the verb *worked*.

> Who read? Answer: She.
> *She* is the subject of the verb *read*.

Subject pronouns are divided into the following categories: The person speaking (the **first person**), the person spoken to (the **second person**), and the person spoken about (the **third person**). These categories are further divided into singular and plural.

SINGULAR	ENGLISH	SPANISH
1st PERSON	*I*	**yo**
the person speaking		
2nd PERSON	*you*	**tú**
the person spoken to		
3rd PERSON	*he*	**él**
the person or object spoken about	*she*	**ella**
	it	
	(you)	**usted**
PLURAL		
1st PERSON	*we*	**nosotros**
the person speaking plus others		**nosotras**
John and *I* speak Spanish.		
we		
2nd PERSON	*you*	**vosotros**
the persons spoken to		**vosotras**
Anita and *you* speak Spanish.		
you		
3rd PERSON	*they*	**ellos**
the persons or objects spoken about		**ellas**
John and *Anita* speak Spanish.		
they	*(you)*	**ustedes**

Let us compare the subject pronouns in English and Spanish.

The English subject pronouns do not always correspond exactly to the Spanish subject pronouns. Let us look at the pronouns that are different so you can learn to choose the correct form.

IT

In English: Whenever you refer to the one thing or idea, you use the pronoun *it*.

>> Where is the book? *It* is on the table.
>> John has an idea. *It* is very interesting.

In Spanish: The subject pronoun *it* is not generally expressed. The verb ending indicates a third person singular; "it" is simply understood especially when the verb refers to a thing or an idea.

>> ¿Dónde está el libro? Está sobre la mesa.

>>> *It* is understod as part of the verb
>>> **está** since it refers to a thing.

>> *Where is the book?* **It** *is on the table.*

>> Juan tiene una idea. Es muy interesante.

>>> *It* is understood as part of the verb
>>> **es** since it refers to an idea.

>> *John has an idea.* **It** *is very interesting.*

WE = **nosotros, nosotras**

In English: The word *we* refers to the person speaking plus others.

>> *John* and *I* are going to the movies.
>> *We* are leaving at 7:00.

In Spanish: There are two forms: **nosotros** and **nosotras**. Nosotros is used when "we" includes all males or a mixed group of males and females. **Nosotras** is used when the "we" includes only females.

> Juan y yo vamos al cine. **Nosotros** salimos a las 7.
> masc.   masc. or fem.   masc. subject
> └────┬────┘   pronoun
>   antecedents

John and I are going to the movies. We are leaving at 7:00.

> María y yo vamos al cine. **Nosotras** salimos a las 7.
> fem.   fem.   fem. subject
> └───┬───┘   pronoun
>   antecedents

Mary and I are going to the movies. We are leaving at 7:00.

THEY = **ellos, ellas**

In English: Whenever you refer to more than one person or object, you use the plural pronoun *they.*

> My brothers play tennis. *They* practice every day.
> My sisters play soccer. *They* practice every day.
> Where are the books? *They* are on the table.

In Spanish: There are two forms: **ellos** and **ellas**. Ellos is used when "they" refers to all males or a mixed group of males and females. **Ellas** is used when "they" refers to all females.

> Mis hermanos juegan al tenis. **Ellos** practican todos los días.
> masc. pl.   masc. pl.
> antecedent   subject pronoun

My brothers play tennis. They practice every day.

Mis hermanas juegan al fútbol. **Ellas** practican todos los días.

fem. pl.   fem. pl.
antecedent   subject pronoun

*My sisters play soccer. **They** practice every day.*

The subject pronoun "they" is not generally expressed when *they* refers to something other than people. The verb ending indicates a third person plural; "they" is simply understood.

¿Dónde están los libros? Están sobre la mesa.

> *They* is understood as part of the verb
> **están** since *they* refers to things.

*Where are the books? **They** are on the table.*

YOU = **tú, usted, vosotros, vosotras, ustedes**

As you can see there are several words for "you" in Spanish. Tú and vosotros/vosotras are 2nd person pronouns; they are called **familiar you**. Usted and ustedes are 3rd person pronouns and are called **formal you**. To help you learn how to choose the correct form of *you* in Spanish an entire section has been devoted to **"What is Meant by Familiar and Formal You?"** (see p. 43).

Practice

A. In the space provided, fill in the English and Spanish subject pronouns that correspond to the PERSON and NUMBER indicated.

		SUBJECT PRONOUN	
PERSON	NUMBER	ENGLISH	SPANISH
1. 3rd	pl.	_____	_____
2. 2nd	sing.	_____	_____
3. 1st	sing.	_____	_____
4. 2nd	pl.	_____	_____
5. 1st	pl.	_____	_____
6. 3rd	sing.	_____	_____

B. Write the Spanish subject pronoun that you would use to replace the words in italics. If no pronoun is needed, write 0 in the space.

SPANISH
SUBJECT PRONOUN

1. *I* am very tired.   _____

2. *It* is very hot outside.   _____

3. Mary and I are leaving tomorrow.   _____

4. My keys? I think *they* are on the table.   _____

5. "Where do your parents live?"
   "*They* live in New Jersey."   _____

6. *Gloria and Anita* are my best friends.   _____

What is Meant by Familiar and Formal *You*?

In English: There is no difference between "you" in the singular and "you" in the plural. If you were in a room with many people and asked aloud, "Are you coming with me?" the "you" could refer to one person or many; it could also refer to close friends or complete strangers, the President of the United States or a dog.

In Spanish: There is a difference between "you" in the singular and "you" in the plural; there is also a difference between the "you" used with close friends, the familiar you, and the "you" used with persons you do not know well, the formal you.

FAMILIAR *YOU* = **tú, vosotros/vosotras**

The familiar forms of *you* are used with members of one's family, friends, children, and pets. In general, you use the familiar forms with persons you call by a first name.

1. To address one person = singular male or female = **tú.**

> Juan, ¿cómo estás tú?
> masculine singular   familiar you

> *John, how are you?*

> María, ¿cómo estás tú?
> feminine singular   familiar you

> *Mary, how are you?*

2. To address more than one person = plural

- a group of all males or a group of males and females = **vosotros**

Juan y Pablo, ¿cómo estáis **vosotros?**
<u>   </u> |
masculine plural   familiar you

*John and Paul, how are **you**?*

Juan y María, ¿cómo estáis **vosotros?**
<u>   </u> |
masculine plural   familiar you

*John and Mary, how are **you**?*

- a group of all females = **vosotras**

María y Ana, ¿cómo estáis **vosotras?**
<u>   </u> |
feminine plural   familiar you

*Mary and Ann, how are **you**?*

NOTE: The plural familiar forms **vosotros** and **vosotras** are used only in Spain. In Latin America **ustedes** is used as the plural of **tú**. See below.

FORMAL *You* = **usted** and **ustedes**

The formal forms of *you* are used to address persons you do not know well or persons to whom you should show respect. In general, you use the formal forms with persons you address with a title: Ms. Smith, Mr. Jones, Dr. Anderson, Professor Gómez.

1. To address one person = singular male or female = **usted**

Señor Gómez, ¿cómo está **usted?**

masculine singular   formal you

Mr. Gómez, how are you?

Señora Gómez, ¿cómo está **usted?**

feminine singular   formal you

Mrs. Gómez, how are you?

2. To address more than one person = plural, a group of males, females or mixed = **ustedes**

Profesor Gómez y Doctor García, ¿cómo están **ustedes?**

formal you   plural

Professor Gómez and Doctor Garía, how are you?

NOTE: In Latin America **ustedes** is the plural of both the familiar and formal forms: **vosotros/vosotras** are not used. In Latin America **ustedes** would be used in the following situations:

Profesor Gómez y Doctor García, ¿cómo están **ustedes?**

formal you   masculine plural

Professor Gómez and Doctor García, how are you?

Juan y María, ¿cómo están **ustedes?**

familiar you   mixed group plural

John and Mary, how are you?

Ana y María, ¿cómo están **ustedes?**

familiar you   feminine plural

Ann and Mary, how are you?

Here is a chart you can use as a reference.

		ENGLISH	SPANISH	
			SPAIN	LATIN AMERICA
FAMILIAR	SINGULAR	you	tú	tú
	PLURAL	you	vosotros vosotras	ustedes
FORMAL	SINGULAR	you	usted	usted
	PLURAL	you	ustedes	ustedes

If you are in doubt as to whether to use the familiar or formal forms, use the formal forms unless speaking to a child or animal. The formal forms of *you* show respect for the person you are talking to and use of familiar forms can be considered rude if you do not know a person well.

TO CHOOSE THE CORRECT FORM OF *YOU*

In order to choose the correct form of *you* in Spanish, you should ask yourself the following questions:

1. Do you need the familiar or formal form?
2. If you need the formal form:
   - Are you speaking to one person?
     Then the form is singular = **usted**
     Are you speaking to more than one person?
     Then the form is plural = **ustedes**

3. If you need the familiar form:
   - Are you speaking to one person?
     Then the form is singular = **tú**
   - Are you speaking to more than one person?
     Then the form is plural, but the plural form you will
     choose depends on the country you are in.
   - Are you in Latin America?
     Then the form is the same as the formal plural form = ustedes
   - Are you in Spain?
     Then the form will depend on the gender of the group
     you are addressing.
       - Are you speaking to a group of all males
         or males and females?
         Then the form is masculine = **vosotros**
       - Are you speaking to a group of all females?
         Then the form is feminine = **vosotras**

Let's find the Spanish equivalent for you in the following sentences.

Mr. President, are you coming with us?

> Familiar or formal: Formal
> Singular or plural: Singular
> Then the form is **usted.**

Señor Presidente, ¿viene **usted** con nosotros?

Mr. and Mrs. Lado, are you coming with us?

> Familiar or formal: Formal
> Singular or plural: Plural
> Then the form is **ustedes.**

Señor y señora Lado, ¿vienen **ustedes** con nosotros?

John, are you coming with us?

> Familiar or formal: Familiar
> Singular or plural: Singular
> Then the form is **tú**

Juan, ¿vienes **tú** con nosotros?

*Isabel and Gloria, are **you** coming with us?*

> Familiar or formal: Familiar
> Singular or plural: Plural
> Spain or Latin America: Spain
> Males or mixed group or all females: Females
> Then the form is **vosotras**

Isabel y Gloria ¿venís **vosotras** con nosotros?

*Vincent and John, are **you** coming with us?*

> Familiar or formal: Familiar
> Singular or plural: Plural
> Spain or Latin America: Latin America
> Then the form is **ustedes.**

Vicente y Juan ¿vienen **ustedes** con nosotros?

Below is a flow chart of the steps you have to follow to find the correct form of "you" in Spanish. It is important that you do the steps in sequence because each step depends on the previous one.

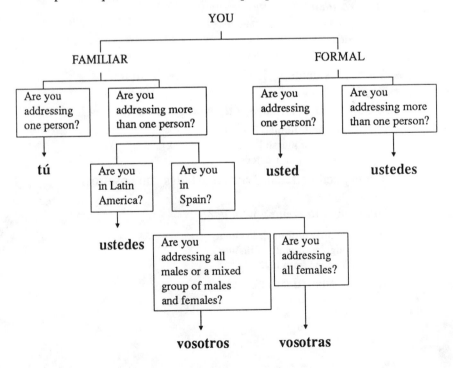

Practice

Write the form of *you* used in Spain and Latin America that would be used to replace the words in italics.

	SPAIN	LATIN AMERICA
1. Mr. and Mrs. Fuentes, how are *you*?	_____	_____
2. Teresa, where are *you* going?	_____	_____
3. Señorita Acosta, will *you* please finish this report?	_____	_____
4. Come on children, *you* must go to bed.	_____	_____
5. Daddy, will *you* play a game with me?	_____	_____
6. Professor Suárez, *you* haven't given us our homework for tomorrow.	_____	_____

What is a Verb Conjugation?

A **verb conjugation** is a list of the six possible forms of the verb for a particular tense. For each tense, there is one verb form for each of the six persons used as the subject of the verb. (See **What is a Subject Pronoun?**, **p. 37**.)

In English: Most verbs change very little. Let us look at the various forms of the verb *to sing* when each of the possible pronouns is the subject.[1]

---

[1]In this section we will talk about the present tense only (see **What is the Present Tense?**, p. 78).

SINGULAR
    1st PERSON   I *sing* with the music.
    2nd PERSON   You *sing* with the music.

    3rd PERSON   { He *sings* with the music.
                                  { She *sings* with the music.
                                  { It *sings* with the music.

PLURAL
    1st PERSON   We *sing* with the music.
    2nd PERSON   You *sing* with the music.
    3rd PERSON   They *sing* with the music.

Conjugating verbs in English is relatively easy because there is only one change in the verb forms; in the 3rd person singular the verb adds an "-s".

In Spanish: Each verb has six different forms in each tense. Therefore, it is necessary to know the form of the verb for each of the six persons in each tense. Memorizing six forms for all the tenses of all verbs that exist would be an impossible and endless task. Fortunately, Spanish verbs belong to one of two categories.

Regular verbs—Verbs whose forms follow a regular pattern; only one example must be memorized and the pattern can then be applied to the other verbs of the same group.

Irregular verbs—Verbs whose forms do not follow any regular pattern and must be memorized individually.

A. SUBJECT

Let us now conjugate in Spanish the verb **cantar** (*to sing*). Pay special attention to the subject.

SINGULAR

1ˢᵗ PERSON	**yo**	canto
2ⁿᵈ PERSON	**tú**	cantas
3ʳᵈ PERSON	**él** **ella** **usted** ⎱	canta

PLURAL

1ˢᵗ PERSON	**nosotros** **nosotras** ⎰	cantamos
2ⁿᵈ PERSON	**vosotros** **vosotras** ⎰	cantáis
3ʳᵈ PERSON	**ellos** **ellas** **ustedes** ⎱	cantan

Each subject represents the doer of the action of the verb.

1ˢᵗ person singular—The *I form* of the verb (the **yo** form) is used whenever the person speaking is the doer of the action.

> **Yo canto** mucho.
> *I sing a lot.*

> Generalmente **yo canto** muy bien.
> *Generally I sing very well.*

Notice that **yo** is not capitalized except as the first word of a sentence.

2ⁿᵈ person singular—the *you familiar form* of the verb (the **tú** form) is used whenever the person spoken to (with whom you are on familiar terms) is the doer of the action.

> Juan, **tú cantas** muy bien.
> *John, you sing very well.*

3rd person singular— the *he, she, you formal form* of the verb (the **él** form) is used when the person or thing spoken about is the doer of the action. The 3rd person singular subject can be expressed in one of four ways.

1. by the third person singular masculine pronoun **él** (*he*) and the third person singular feminine pronoun **ella** (*she*):

> **El canta** muy bien.
> *He sings very well.*

> **Ella canta** muy bien.
> *She sings very well.*

2. by the singular pronoun **usted** (*you*):

> Señor Gómez, **usted canta** muy bien.
> *Mr. Gómez, you sing very well.*

> Señorita Gómez, **usted canta** muy bien.
> *Miss Gómez, you sing very well.*

NOTE: The pronoun **usted** is generally abbreviated as **Ud.** The abbreviation is used far more frequently than the entire word.

3. by one proper name:

> María **canta** muy bien.
> *Mary sings very well.*

> Pedro **canta** muy bien.
> *Pedro sings very well.*

> El señor García **canta** muy bien.
> *Mr. García sings very well.*

4. by a singular noun:

> El hombre **canta** muy bien.
> *The man sings very well.*

> La niña **canta** muy bien.
> *The girl sings very well.*

> El pájaro **canta** muy bien.
> *The bird sings very well.*

NOTE: The subject pronoun *it* has no Spanish equivalent. *It* as a subject is generally not expressed but rather understood as part of the verb. (See **What is a Subject Pronoun?**, p. 37.)

> *John has a new car. **It's (it is)** very nice.*
> Juan tiene un coche nuevo. **Es** muy lindo.

> > *It* is understood as part of the verb *es.*

1ˢᵗ person plural—The *we form* of the verb (the **nosotros** form) is used whenever "I" (the speaker) is one of the doers of the action; that is, whenever the speaker is included in a plural or multiple subject.

> Isabel, Gloria y yo **cantamos** muy bien.
> *Isabel, Gloria and I sing very well.*

> > In this sentence *Isabel, Gloria and I* could be replaced by the pronoun *we,* so that in Spanish you must use the **nosotros** form of the verb.

2ⁿᵈ person plural—The *you familiar plural form* of the verb (the **vosotros** form) is used only in Spain when you are speaking to two or more persons with whom you would use **tú** individually.

> Juan y tú **cantáis muy bien.**
> *Juan and you sing very well.*

> > In this sentence *John* (whom you would address with the **tú** form) and *you* could be replaced by the pronoun *you,* so that in Spanish you must use the **vosotros** form of the verb.

Many beginning Spanish textbooks do not emphasize or practice the **vosotros** form. Your instructor will inform you if you need to learn the **vosotros** forms of verbs or not.

3rd person plural—The *they* or *you formal form* of the verb (the **ellos** form) is used when the persons or things spoken about are the doers of the action. The 3rd person plural subject can be expressed in one of five ways:

1. by the third person plural masculine pronoun **ellos** (*they*) and the third person plural feminine pronoun **ellas** (*they*):

    Ellos cantan muy bien.
    They sing very well.

    Ellas cantan muy bien.
    They sing very well.

2. by the plural pronoun **ustedes** (*you*):

    Señor y señora García, **ustedes cantan** muy bien.
    Mr. and Mrs. García, you sing very well.

    NOTE: The pronoun **ustedes** is generally abbreviated as **Uds.** The abbreviation is used far more frequently than the entire word.

3. by two or more names:

    Isabel, Gloria y Roberto **cantan** muy bien.
    ellos

    Isabel, Gloria and Robert sing very well.

    In this sentence *Isabel, Gloria and Robert* could be replaced by *they* so that in Spanish you must use the **ellos** form of the verb.

La señora Gómez y la señora Jiménez **cantan** muy bien.

ellas

Mrs. Gómez and Mrs. Jiménez sing very well.

> In this sentence *Mrs. Gómez and Mrs. Jiménez*
> could be replaced by *they* so that in Spanish
> you must use the **ellos** form of the verb.

4. by two or more singular nouns:

La chica y su padre **cantan** muy bien.

ellos

The girl and her father sing very well.

> In this sentence *the girl and her father* could be
> replaced by *they* so that in Spanish you must use
> the **ellos** form of the verb.

5. by a plural noun:

Las chicas **cantan** muy bien.
The girls sing very well.

NOTE: The subject pronoun *they* referring to things is generally not expressed but rather understood as part of the verb. (See **What is a Subject Pronoun?**, p. 37.)

*Mary has new shoes. **They are** very nice.*
María tiene zapatos nuevos. **Son** muy lindos.

> *They* is understood as part of the
> verb **son** since it refers to a thing.

B. VERB FORM

Let us again look at the conjugation of the same verb *to sing*, paying special attention to the verb forms. Notice that each of the six persons has a different verb form. However, when two or more pronouns belong to the same person, there is only one verb form, for instance, the 3rd person singular has three pronouns; **él, ella,** and **Ud.** but they all have the same verb form: **canta.**

yo	canto
tú	cantas
él	
ella	canta
Ud.	
nosotros	cantamos
nosotras	
vosotros	cantáis
vosotros	
ellos	
ellas	cantan
Uds.	

The Spanish verb is composed of two parts.

1. The **stem** (also called the **root)** is formed by dropping the last two letters from the infinitive.

INFINITIVE	STEM
cantar	cant-
comer	com-
vivir	viv-

The stem will usually not change throughout a conjugation. However, in certain verbs called **stem-changing verbs,** the stem will change in a minor way.

2. The **ending** changes for each person in the conjugation of regular and irregular verbs. You will know which endings to add when you have established which group the verb belongs to.

C. VERB GROUPS

Regular verbs are divided into three groups, also called **conjugations.** The groups are identified according to the infinitive endings.

1st GROUP	2nd GROUP	3rd GROUP
-ar	-er	-ir

Each of the three verb groups has its own set of endings for each tense (see **What is Meant by Tense?**, p. 75). You will need to learn the forms of only one sample verb from each group in order to conjugate any regular verb belonging to that group. As an example, let us look more closely at regular -ar verbs, that is, verbs like **hablar** (*to speak*) and **tomar** (*to take*) that follow the pattern of **cantar** (*to sing*) conjugated above.

1. Identify the verb group by its infinitive endings.

> hablar
> tomar   -ar verbs

2. Find the verb stem by removing the infinitive endings.

> habl-
> tom-

3. Add the ending that corresponds to the subject.

yo	hablo	yo	tomo
tú	hablas	tú	tomas
él ella Ud.	habla	él ella Ud.	toma
nosotros nosotras	hablamos	nosotros nosotras	tomamos
vosotros vosotras	habláis	vosotros vosotras	tomáis
ellos ellas Uds.	hablan	ellos ellas Uds.	toman

The endings for **-er** and **-ir** verbs will be different but the process of conjugation is always the same for regular verbs:

1. Identify the group of the verb by its infinitive ending.
2. Find the verb stem.
3. According to the group, add the ending that corresponds to the subject.

OMITTING THE SUBJECT PRONOUN

As you can see, in Spanish the verb ending indicates the subject. For instance, **hablo** can only have **yo** as a subject. Similarly, the subject of **hablas** can only be **tú**; the subject of **hablamos, nosotros**; the subject of **habláis, vosotros**.

Since you know the subject from the verb form, the subject pronoun is often omitted.

hablo	=	*I speak*
hablas	=	*you speak*
hablamos	=	*we speak*
habláis	=	*you speak*

If you do include the subject pronoun, it adds strong emphasis to the subject.

Yo canto. = *I sing (but he doesn't).*
Nosotros cantamos. = *We sing (but they don't).*

However, in the third person singular and plural it is often necessary to include the pronoun in order to avoid any doubt about who is the subject of the verb.

	él habla	*he speaks*
habla could be	ella habla	*she speaks*
	Ud. habla	*you speak*

	ellos hablan	*they speak*
hablan could be	ellas hablan	*they speak*
	Uds. hablan	*you speak*

The subject pronouns are included to clear up or clarify who is the subject in the above examples.

NOTE: In many textbooks only the pronoun **nosotros** (instead of both **nosotros** and **nosotras**) will be listed in conjugations of new verbs. Likewise, only **vosotros** (instead of both **vosotros** and **vosotras**) will be listed.

Practice

A. This is the regular verb **comer** (*to eat*) conjugated in the present tense.

	COMER		
yo	como	nosotros	comemos
tú	comes	vosotros	coméis
él		ellos	
ella	come	ellas	comen
Ud.		Uds.	

- Circle the stem of the verb above.
- Draw a box around the ending for each person of the verb above.
- Now conjugate the regular verb **beber** (*to drink*) by filling in the spaces below.

yo _____   nosotros _____

tú _____   vosotros _____

él
ella _____   ellos
ellas _____
Ud.   Uds.

B. This is the verb **escribir** (*to write*) conjugated in the present tense.

	ESCRIBIR		
yo	escribo	nosotros	escribimos
tú	escribes	vosotros	escribís
él		ellos	
ella	escribe	ellas	escriben
Ud.		Uds.	

- Circle the stem of the verb above.
- Draw a box around the ending for each person of the verb above.
- Now conjugate the regular verb **vivir** (*to live*) by filling in the spaces below.

yo _____   nosotros _____

tú _____   vosotros _____

él
ella _____
Ud.

ellos
ellas _____
Uds.

What are Affirmative and Negative Sentences?

A sentence can be classified as to whether it states that a fact or situation is or is not true.

An **affirmative sentence** states that a fact or situation is true; it *affirms* the information it contains.

> Spain is a country in Europe.
> John will work in the university.
> They liked to travel.

A **negative sentence** states that a fact or a situation is not true; it denies or *negates* the information it contains. A negative sentence includes a word of negation such as *no, not,* or *nobody*.

> Spain is *not* a country in Asia.
> John will *not* work in a factory.
> They did *not* like to travel.

In English: An affirmative sentence can become a negative sentence in one of two ways:

1. by adding the word **not** after certain verbs.

AFFIRMATIVE	NEGATIVE
John is a student.	John is *not* a student.
Mary can do it.	Mary can*not* do it.
They will travel.	They will *not* travel.

Frequently, the word *not* is attached to the verb and the letter "o" is replaced by an apostrophe; this new word is called a **contraction**.

> John *isn't* a student.
> |
> is not

> Mary *can't* do it.
> |
> cannot

> They *won't* travel.
> |
> will not

Note that the contraction of *will not* is *won't*.

2. by adding the auxiliary verb **do, does,** or **did** + **not** + the dictionary form of the main verb. (*Do* or *does* is used for negatives in the present tense and *did* for negatives in the past tense. (See **What is the Present Tense?**, p. 78 and **What is the Past Tense?**, p. 80.)

AFFIRMATIVE	NEGATIVE
We study a lot.	We *do not study* a lot.
Julia writes well.	Julia *does not write* well.
The plane arrived.	The plane *did not arrive.*

Frequently *do, does,* or *did* form a contraction with *not: don't, doesn't,* or *didn't.*

In Spanish: The basic rule for turning an affirmative sentence into a negative sentence is much more simple than in English. You merely place **no** in front of the conjugated verb.

AFFIRMATIVE	NEGATIVE
Estudiamos mucho.	**No** estudiamos mucho.
We study a lot.	*We **do not** study a lot.*
Julia escribe bien.	Julia **no** escribe bien.
Julia writes well.	*Julia **doesn't** write well.*
El avión ha llegado.	El avión **no** ha llegado.
The plane arrived.	*The plane **didn't** arrive.*

Remember that there is no equivalent for the auxiliary verbs *do, does,* or *did* in Spanish; do not try to include them in a negative sentence.

NEGATIVE ANSWERS

When answering a question negatively in English, both *no* and *not* will often appear in the answer.

> *Do you live near the park?*
> *No, I do not live near the park.*

Since both *no* and *not* have the Spanish equivalent **no,** the word **no** will appear twice in the negative answer to that question in Spanish.

¿Vives cerca del parque?
No, no vivo cerca del parque.

no not   The first **no** answers the question; it has the English
equivalent of *no*. The second **no** accompanies the
verb; it has the English equivalent of *not*.

Practice

A. The following sentences are affirmative. Write the negative of each
English sentence on the line below.

1. We want to leave class early.

_____

2. He did his homework yesterday.

_____

3. Teresa will go to Chile this summer.

_____

4. Robert can go to the restaurant with us.

_____

5. Mr. Smith plays tennis every day.

_____

B. Re-read the sentences you have just written. Circle the elements that
indicate the negative.

C. Put an X over the words that would not appear in the Spanish
negative sentence.

What are Declarative and Interrogative Sentences?

A sentence can be classified according to its purpose.

A **declarative sentence** is a sentence that is a statement; it *declares* the information.

> Columbus discovered America in 1492.

An **interrogative sentence** is a sentence that asks a question.

> When did Columbus discover America?

In written language, an interrogative sentence always ends with a question mark.

In English: A declarative sentence can be changed to an interrogative sentence in one of two ways:

1. by adding the auxiliary verb *do, does,* or *did* before the subject and changing the main verb to the dictionary form of the verb (*do* and *does* are used to introduce a question in the present tense and *did* to introduce a question in the past tense—see **What is the Present Tense?**, p. 78 and **What is the Past Tense?**, p. 80).

DECLARATIVE ⟶	INTERROGATIVE
Philip *likes* sports cars.	*Does* Philip *like* sports cars?
Paul and Mary *sing* together.	*Do* Paul and Mary *sing* together?
Mark *went* to Lima.	*Did* Mark *go* to Lima?

2. by inverting or switching the normal word order of subject + verb so the word order in the question is verb + subject

DECLARATIVE ⟶	INTERROGATIVE
Paul is home.	*Is Paul* home?
verb	subject
subject	verb

I am late.
       verb
subject

Am I late?
       subject
verb

She will come tomorrow.
       verb
subect

Will she come tomorrow?
       subject
       verb

In Spanish: A declarative sentence is changed to an interrogative sentence by placing the subject after the verb. The word order of the question is verb + subject.

STATEMENT	QUESTION
Juan estudia.	¿Estudia Juan?
John studies.	*Does John study?*
Los niños cantan.	¿Cantan los niños?
The children sing.	*Do the children sing?*

Notice that in written Spanish the question is signalled at both the beginning and end of the sentence. The punctuation mark at the beginning of the sentence looks like an upside-down question mark (¿); a question mark like the one in English is located at the end of the sentence (?).

Be sure to ignore the auxiliary verbs *do/does/did* when using Spanish. Spanish has no such helping verbs.

When a statement consists of a subject and verb plus one or two words, those few words are usually placed between the subject and the verb. The word order of the question is verb + remainder + subject.

STATEMENT	QUESTION
Juan estudia español.	¿Estudia español Juan?
subject verb remainder	verb remainder subject
John studies Spanish.	*Does John study Spanish?*
La casa es grande.	¿Es grande la casa?
subject verb remainder	verb remainder subject
The house is big.	*Is the house big?*
Los niños cantan bien.	¿Cantan bien los niños?
subject verb remainder	verb remainder subject
The children sing well.	*Do the children sing well?*

TAG QUESTIONS

In both English and Spanish you can transform a statement into a question by adding a short phrase to the end of the statement. This short phrase is called a **tag** or a **tag question**. Tag questions are used when you expect a yes or no answer to the question.

In English: The tag question repeats the idea of the statement in a negative way.

> John is a nice guy, *isn't he?*
> We study a lot, *don't we?*

In Spanish: The words **¿no?**, **¿verdad?**, or **¿no es verdad?** can be added to the end of a statement to form a tag question.

> Juan es un buen chico, **¿no?**
> *John is a nice guy, **isn't he**?*
>
> Trabajas mucho, **¿verdad?**
> *You work hard, **don't you**?*

Hoy es miércoles, ¿no es verdad?
Today is Wednesday, isn't it?

Practice

A. The following are declarative sentences. Write the interrogative of each sentence on the line below.

1   Richard and Kathy studied all evening.

_____

2. Your brother eats a lot.

_____

3. The girl's parents speak Spanish.

_____

B. Read the questions you have just written. Circle the English words that indicate the interrogative.
C. Put an X over the words that would not appear in the Spanish interrogative sentence.
D. Draw a line under the words that would be the last words of the Spanish question.

What are Some Equivalents of *To Be*?

In English: The verb *to be* has the following forms in the present tense: *I am; you are; he/she/it is; we are; you are; they are.* It is used in a variety of ways:

- for telling time

    It is 4:00.

- for discussing health

    John isn't very well.

- for describing traits and characteristics

    Mary is tall and blond.

- for telling ages

    I am twenty years old.

- for explaining what there is or there are in specific places

    There are twenty-five students in the class.

In Spanish: There are various verbs used to express the English verb
to be:

ENGLISH	SPANISH
	1. **ser** (*to be*)
to be	2. **estar** (*to be*)
	3. **tener** (*to have*)
there is, there are	4. **hay** (a form of *to have*)

Depending on what you want to say, you will have to use one of
these four verbs. Here are a few rules to help you select the correct
one:

1. SER = *to be*

• to tell time

> *It is four o' clock.*
> |
> time

> **Son** las cuatro.

• to show possession

> *That car is John's.*
> |
> possession

> Ese coche **es** de Juan.

> *This book is yours.*
> |
> possession

> Este libro **es** tuyo.

• to express nationality and origin

> *Mary is Spanish; she is from Madrid.*
> |　　　　　　　　　　|
> nationality　　　　　　origin

> María **es** española; **es** de Madrid.

• with nouns to identify someone or something

> *Mr. Robles is an engineer.*
> |
> noun of identification

> El señor Robles **es** ingeniero.

That building is the language laboratory.
        └────────┬────────┘
          noun of identification

Ese edificio **es** el laboratorio de lenguas.

• with adjectives to describe traits or characteristics
  (See **What is an Adjective?**, p. 132.)

Mary is tall and blond.
        └────┬────┘
     adjectives describing traits

María **es** alta y rubia.

2. ESTAR = *to be*

• to express location

John is in the library.
        └────┬────┘
         location

Juan **está** en la biblioteca.

The books are on the table.
        └────┬────┘
         location

Los libros **están** sobre la mesa.

• to discuss health

How are you?
 └──┬──┘
asking about health

¿Cómo **está** Ud.?

Mary is fine but John is sick.
        └────┬────┘
      describing health

María **está** bien pero Juan **está** enfermo.

- with adjectives that describe a condition

> *I am tired and worried.*
> └────┬────┘
> adjectives of condition

Estoy cansada y preocupada.

SER VS. ESTAR

The only situation in which both **ser** and **estar** can be used is when the verb *to be* is followed by an adjective. You will need to decide what type of adjective is used in order to correctly select a form of **ser** or **estar**.

- adjectives that describe traits and characteristics = SER

> *My house is yellow.*
> |
> trait

Mi casa **es** amarilla.
|
ser

> Ser is used because the adjective *yellow* distinguishes the house from others. It answers the question, Which house is yours?

> *Mary is thin.*
> |
> trait

María **es** delgada.
|
ser

> Ser is used because the adjective *thin* distinguishes Mary from other females. It answers the question, Which person is Mary?

- adjectives that describe conditions = ESTAR

> *My house **is** dirty.*
> |
>   condition

Mi casa **está** sucia.
         |
       estar

> **Estar** is used because the adjective *dirty*
> describes a special condition, not a normal
> characteristic of the house. It answers the
> question, What condition is the house in?

> *Mary **is** tired.*
> |
>   condition

María **está** cansada.
         |
       estar

> **Estar** is used because the adjective *tired*
> describes a special condition not a normal
> characteristic of Mary. It answers the question,
> What is Mary's condition?

3. TENER = *To have, to be*

The verb **tener** (*to have*) is sometimes used in expressions where English uses the verb *to be*. These expressions using **tener** must be memorized. Here are a few examples:

> *I **am** hungry.*   *I **am** twenty years old.*
> | |
> to be   to be
>
> **Tengo** hambre.   **Tengo** veinte años.
> | |
> to have   to have
> "I have hunger"   "I have twenty years"

4. HAY = *there is/there are*

The English expressions *there is* or *there are* are translated with the Spanish word **hay. Hay** is used to explain the presence or absence of people or things in a particular place. **Hay** is invariable, that is, it does not change form since it can be either singular or plural.

> *There is a book on the table.*
> |
>   singular noun
>
> **Hay** un libro sobre la mesa.

> *There are many books on the table.*
> |
>   plural noun
>
> **Hay** muchos libros sobre la mesa.

You must learn to use this very common expression correctly and avoid using **estar** when you shouldn't. To avoid using the wrong form, see if you can replace the "is" or "are" of the English sentence with "there is" or "there are". If you can, you must use **hay;** if you can't, then **está** or **están** must be used to show location.

> On the table *is* a book
> |
>   hay
>   You can say: On the table *there is* a book.
>
> The book *is* on the table.
> |
>   está
>   You can't say: The book *there is* on the table.
>
> In the classroom *are* students.
> |
>   hay
>   You can say: In the classroom *there are* students.
>
> The chairs and tables *are* in the classroom.
> |
>   están
>   You can't say: The chairs and tables
>   *there are* in the classroom.

Practice

A. Decide if the *italicized* words are adjectives that describe a characteristic (CHAR) or a condition (COND). Then write the infinitive form of the verb you would use in Spanish.

	ADJECTIVE	INFINITIVE
1. My car is *gray*.	CHAR COND	_____
2. My car is *dirty*.	CHAR COND	_____
3. The students are *worried*.	CHAR COND	_____
4. John is *tall, dark,* and *handsome*.	CHAR COND	_____
5. I am *bored*.	CHAR COND	_____
6. John, are you *sick?*	CHAR COND	_____
7. Mary and I are *blond*.	CHAR COND	_____

B. Using the rules outlined above decide if **ser** or **estar** would be used as the Spanish equivalent of the forms of *to be*.
   • Circle you choice.

1. That car is my friend's.	SER	ESTAR
2. Hi. How are you?	SER	ESTAR
3. Where is Carol?	SER	ESTAR
4. It is 5:30.	SER	ESTAR
5. Your coat is in your room.	SER	ESTAR
6. Professor Marín is Colombian.	SER	ESTAR
7. My father is a chemist.	SER	ESTAR
8. John is from Michigan.	SER	ESTAR

C. Using the rules outlined above decide if **estar** or **hay** would be used as the verbs in the following sentences in Spanish.
   • Circle your choice.

1. There are twenty-five students
   in my Spanish class.   ESTAR   HAY

2. The students are in the
   Spanish class.   ESTAR   HAY

3. Is there any sugar on the table? ESTAR   HAY

4. Where is my umbrella?   ESTAR   HAY

5. Right now there is only one
   person in the room.   ESTAR   HAY

What is Meant by Tense?

The **tense** of a verb indicates the time when the action of the verb takes place, for example, in the present time, in the past, or in the future.

I am studying.	PRESENT
I studied.	PAST
I will study.	FUTURE

As you can see in the above examples, just by putting the verb in a different tense and without giving any additional information (such as "I am studying *now*," "I studied *yesterday*," "I will study *tomorrow*"), you can indicate when the action of the verb takes place.

Tenses may be classified according to the way they are formed. A **simple tense** consists of only one verb form while a **compound tense** consists of two or more verb forms.

In English: There are only two simple tenses: the present and the past.

I study	PRESENT
I studied	PAST

All of the other tenses including the examples below are compound tenses formed by one or more auxiliary verbs (see **What are Auxiliary Verbs?**, p. 28) plus the main verb.

I have studied	PRESENT PERFECT
I was studying	PAST PROGRESSIVE
I will study	FUTURE
I will have studied	FUTURE PERFECT
I would study	CONDITIONAL[1]
I would have studied	CONDITIONAL PERFECT

In Spanish: There are more simple tenses than in English.[1]

estudio	PRESENT
estudié	PRETERITE
estudiaba	IMPERFECT
estudiaré	FUTURE
estudiaría	CONDITIONAL[1]

There are also compound tenses in Spanish. They are formed with the helping verbs **estar** or **haber** + the main verb. Some examples of compound tenses follow.

estoy estudiando	*I am studying*	PRESENT PROGRESSIVE
estaba estudiando	*I was studying*	PAST PROGRESSIVE
he estudiado	*I have studied*	PRESENT PERFECT
había estudiado	*I had studied*	PAST PERFECT
habré estudiado	*I will have studied*	FUTURE PERFECT
habría estudiado	*I would have studied*	CONDITIONAL PERFECT

---

[1] We have included the conditional because it is conjugated like a verb tense, but we have omitted the subjunctive because it has no parallel in English.

These compound tenses are discussed in separate sections of the book: **What is a Progressive Tense?**, p. 89; **What are the Perfect Tenses?**, p. 104.

Practice

Fill in the blanks.

The word tense refers to the (1) _____ an action

takes place. A (2) _____ tense consists of one verb

form; a compound tense consists of (3) _____ or

more verb forms; the (4) _____ verb (or verbs) plus

the (5) _____ verb. The (6) _____

and the (7) _____ tenses are examples of two

simple tenses in English. Spanish has more (8) _____

tenses than English. For instance, the (9) _____ is

a (10) _____ tense in Spanish and a compound

tense in English.

What is the Present Tense?

The **present tense** indicates that the action is happening at the present time. It can be:

when the speaker is speaking	I *see* you.
a habitual action	He *smokes* when he is nervous.
a general truth	The sun *shines* every day.

In English: There are three forms of the verb that indicate the present tense although they have slightly different meanings.

Mary *studies* in the library.	PRESENT
Mary *is studying* in the library.	PRESENT PROGRESSIVE
Mary *does study* in the library.	PRESENT EMPHATIC

When you answer the following questions, you will automatically choose one of the above forms.

Where does Mary study?
Mary *studies* in the library.

Where is Mary studying?
Mary *is studying* in the library.

Does Mary study in the library?
Yes, Mary *does study* in the library.

In Spanish: There is only one verb form to indicate the present tense. It is used to express the meaning of the English present, present progressive, and present emphatic tenses. In Spanish the idea of the present tense is indicated by the ending of the verb, without any auxiliary verb such as *is* and *does*. It is very important, therefore, not to translate these English auxiliary verbs. Simply put the main verb in the present tense.

*Mary **studies** in the library.*
|
estudia

*Mary **is studying** in the library.*
└─┬─┘
estudia

*Mary **does study** in the library.*
└─┬─┘
estudia

Practice

A. The following are questions in a present tense. Complete the answers with a form of the verb *to read* in English.

1. What does Mary do all day?

   She _____.

2. Has she read *Don Quixote?*

   No, but she _____ it right now.

3. Does Mary read Spanish?

   Yes, she _____ Spanish but not French.

B. In Spanish, the answer to question 1 above is the verb form **lee**, from the verb **leer** (*to read*).
   • In the spaces provided write the Spanish verb form for the answers to questions 2 and 3.

   2. _____   3. _____

What is the Past Tense?

The **past tense** is used to express an action that occured in the past.

In English: There are several forms that indicate that the action took place in the past.

I worked	SIMPLE PAST
I was working	PAST PROGRESSIVE
I used to work	WITH HELPING VERB used to
I did work	PAST EMPHATIC
I have worked	PRESENT PERFECT
I had worked	PAST PERFECT

The simple past is called "simple" because it is a simple tense, i.e., it consists of one word (*worked* in the example above). The other past tenses are compound tenses; i.e., they consist of more than one word (*was working, did work*, etc.). The present and past perfect tenses are discussed in a separate section (see **What are the Perfect Tenses?**, p. 104).

In Spanish: There are several verb tenses that can be used to express an action that occurred in the past. Each tense has its own set of endings and its own rules that tell us when and how to use it. We are concerned here with only two of the past tenses in Spanish: the **preterite** (el pretérito) and the **imperfect** (el imperfecto).

A. THE PRETERITE

The preterite is formed by adding certain endings to the stem. There are many irregular verbs in the preterite tense. It is very important to learn the preterite forms given in your textbook since the stems of the preterite are also used to form other verb tenses.

The preterite generally translates as the simple past in English.

hablé	=	*I spoke*
estudié	=	*I studied*

B. The Imperfect

The imperfect is also formed by adding a set of endings to the stem. The conjugation is so regular (there are only three irregular verbs in the imperfect tense) that there is no need to repeat what is in your Spanish textbook. There are two English verb forms that indicate that the imperfect should be used in Spanish.

1. If the English verb form includes, or could include, the expression *used to*.

> *When I was small, I **played** in the park.*
>
>> *I played* could be replaced by *I used to play;* therefore, the Spanish verb is put into the imperfect.
>
> Cuando yo era joven, **jugaba** en el parque.
>>> imperfect

2. If the English form is in the past progressive tense, as in *was playing, were studying*.

> *I **was studying** in my room.*
> Yo **estudiaba** en mi cuarto.

Except for these two verb forms, the English verb will not indicate to you whether you should use the imperfect or the preterite.

Imperfect or Preterite

When discussing and describing past events and activities both the imperfect and preterite are used. You will have to learn to analyze sentences and their context so that you can decide which of the two tenses to use.

For instance, let us look at the English sentence "Robert went out with Mary". The same form of the verb, namely "went out," is used in the following two answers, even though the verb has two different meanings.

1. QUESTION: What did Robert do yesterday?
   ANSWER: He went out with Mary.

   > In this context you are focusing on a single action on one day. The key word in the question is "yesterday."

2. QUESTION: With whom did Robert go out when he was in high school?
   ANSWER: He went out with Mary.

   > In this context you are focusing on a repetitive action over a long period of time; you are saying that Robert *used to go out* with Mary. The key phrase in the question is "when he was in high school."

To translate "Robert went out with Mary" into Spanish you need to know the context in which the verb is used (1 or 2 above) since the Spanish verb "went out" is in a different tense in each example.

1. Roberto **salió** con María.

   preterite

   Use of the preterite explains what Robert did once during a fixed time period.

2. Roberto **salía** con María.

   imperfect

   Use of the imperfect describes what Robert used to do repeatedly over a period of time.

Remember that since the imperfect and the preterite both take place at the same time in the past, these two tenses are often used to compare the duration of one action to the duration of another action in the same sentence or story. The imperfect is used for the longer of the two actions. To help you choose the correct tense, ask the question "What happened?" The answer will require a verb in the preterite. The answer to the question "What was going on?" will require a verb in the imperfect.

I was reading when he came in.

> Both actions are taking place at the same time. The action
> of *reading* was going on when the *coming in* happened.

Leía cuando **entró.**

imperfect   preterite

Your Spanish textbook will give you additional guidelines to help
you choose the appropriate tense. You should practice analyzing
English paragraphs. Locate the verbs in a past tense and indicate
whether it would be in the imperfect or preterite in Spanish. Occasionally both tenses are possible but one of the two will be more
logical.

Practice

A. Fill in the blanks.

The (1) _____ and the (2) _____

are two examples of the Spanish past tense. Both are

(3) _____ tenses. The (4) _____

focuses on explaining what happened at a particular time in the past.

The (5) _____ focuses on describing what was

going on over a period of time in the past.

B. The following sentences contain verbs in a past tense.
   - Circle the verbs that would be in the imperfect in Spanish.
   - Underline the verbs that would be in the preterite in Spanish.

1. When I was little, I played outdoors a lot.

2. What did you do last summer?

3. When we came home, our mother was watching TV.

4. I used to go to the movies a lot.

5. John had an accident and broke his leg.

6. In the Old West people traveled by stage coach.

What is a Participle?

A **participle** has two functions: (1) It is a form of the verb that is used in combination with an auxiliary verb to indicate certain tenses. (2) It may be used as an adjective or modifier to describe something.

> I was *writing* a letter.
> auxiliary participle

> The *broken* vase was on the floor.
> participle describing *vase*

There are two types of participles: the **present participle** and the **past participle**. As you will learn in your study of Spanish, participles are not always used in the same way in the two languages.

A. THE PRESENT PARTICIPLE

In English: The present participle is easy to recognize because it is the
-ing form of the verb: *working, studying, dancing, playing.*

The present participle is used:

- as an adjective

> This is an *amazing* discovery.
> |
> describes the noun *discovery*

> He was a good *dancing* partner.
> |
> describes the noun *partner*

- in a verbal function

1. as the main verb in compound tenses (see **What is a Progressive Tense?**, p. 89 and **What are the Perfect Tenses?**, p. 104)

> She is *singing*.
> |
> present progressive of *to sing*

> They were *dancing*.
> |
> past progressive of *to dance*

2. in a participial phrase after a preposition

> After *eating* dinner, we went to the movies.
> |
> preposition |
> participle

> Philip learned English by *studying* hard.
> |
> preposition |
> participle

In Spanish: The present participle is formed by adding **-ando** to the stem of **-ar** verbs and **-iendo** to the stem of **-er** and **-ir** verbs. The **-ndo** of the Spanish participle corresponds to the *-ing* of the English present participle.

INFINITIVE	STEM	PRESENT PARTICIPLE
cantar	cant-	**cantando**
comer	com-	**comiendo**
vivir	viv-	**viviendo**

There are some irregular forms that you will have to memorize individually. The present participle is used primarily in the formation of the progressive tenses. (See **What is a Progressive Tense?**, p. 89.)

NOTE: Never assume that an English word ending in *-ing* will translate by its Spanish counterpart in **-ndo**. For example, after prepositions (see **What is a Preposition?**, p. 167) Spanish uses the infinitive form of the verb while English uses a participle in that position.

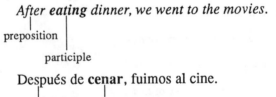

B. THE PAST PARTICIPLE

In English: The past participle is formed in several ways. You can always find it by remembering the form of the verb that follows *I have: I have **spoken**, I have **written**, I have **walked**.*

The past participle is used:

- as an adjective

    Is the *written* word more important than the *spoken* word?

    describes the noun *word*   describes the noun *word*

- as a verb form in combination with the auxiliary verb *have*

    I *have written* all that I have to say.
    He *hasn't spoken* to me since our quarrel.

In Spanish: The past participle of regular verbs is formed using the following pattern:

    -ar verbs add -ado to the stem
    -er and -ir verbs add -ido to the stem

INFINITIVE	STEM	PAST PARTICIPLE
hablar	habl-	hablado
comer	com-	comido
vivir	viv-	vivido

You will have to memorize irregular past participles individually. As you can see from the following examples, the past participle may be very different from the infinitive.

INFINITIVE	PAST PARTICIPLE
decir	dicho
escribir	escrito
poner	puesto
romper	roto

As in English the past participle can be used as an adjective or a verb form.

When the past participle is used as an adjective, it must agree with the noun it modifies in gender and number.

the **closed** *door*

> *Closed* modifies the noun *door*. Since **la puerta**
> (*door*) is feminine singular, the word for *closed* must
> be feminine singular. The participle must end -a.

la puerta **cerrada**

the **broken** *records*

> *Broken* modifies the noun *records*. Since **los discos**
> (*records*) is masculine plural, the word for *broken* must
> be masculine plural. The participle must end in -os.

los discos **rotos**

The most important use of the past participle in Spanish is as a verb
form in combination with the auxiliary verb **haber** to indicate a
perfect tense (see **What are the Perfect Tenses?**, p. 104).

Practice

A. Fill in the blanks.

In English the (1) "-_____" form of the verb as in

"singing" is an example of the (2) _____ participle.

The (3) _____ participle is the form of the verb

following "I have". *Begun* is an example of a (4) _____

participle. In Spanish the (5) _____ participle is

used to form the progressive tense and the (6) _____

participle is used to form the perfect tenses.

B. Determine the Spanish verb form for the words in *italics* and then circle PRES (present participle), PAST (past participle) or INF (infinitive).

1. At 10:00 p.m. John was *watching* TV.   PRES   PAST   INF

2. We had already *gone* when Tom called.   PRES   PAST   INF

3. Barbara finished her homework before *going* out.   PRES   PAST   INF

4. An antique dealer near our house fixes
   broken dolls and toys.   PRES   PAST   INF

5. What are you *doing?*   PRES   PAST   INF

What is a Progressive Tense?

The **progressive tenses** are used to talk about actions that are in progress at a specific moment in time; they emphasize the moment that an action takes place.

> John *is talking* on the phone. (Right now.)
> We *were trying* to start the car. (At that moment.)

In English: The progressive tenses are made up of the auxiliary verb *to be* + the present participle of the main verb.

> We *are leaving* right now.

present participle

present tense of
to be

> At that moment John *was washing* his car.

present participle

past tense of
to be

Notice that it is the tense of the auxiliary verb *to be* that indicates when the action of the main verb takes place.

In Spanish: The progressive tenses are made up of the auxiliary verb **estar** + the present participle of the main verb. A progressive form of the verb exists for all the tenses in Spanish. However, we shall here be concerned only with the present progressive. The present progressive is made up of the present tense of **estar** + the present participle of the main verb.

> **Estamos saliendo** ahora mismo.
> present tense   present participle
> of estar
>
> *We are leaving right now.*

> **¿Estás comiendo** ahora?
> present tense   present participle
> of estar
>
> *Are you eating now?*

PRESENT VS. PROGRESSIVE TENSE

In English: The progressive tenses are used far more frequently in English than in Spanish. They are used to describe habitual actions, to state general truths, and to describe an action that is happening at a specific moment.

In Spanish: The progressive tenses are used only to emphasize an action that is happening at a particular moment or to stress the continuity of an action. The Spanish progressive tenses cannot be used to describe habitual action or to state general truths.

• *John, what are you studying in school?*
  ⌞___⌟

  estudias
  present tense

  > The present tense is used because you are asking what
  > John is studying in general over a period of time.

• *John, what are you studying now?*
  ⌞___⌟

  estás estudiando
  present progressive

  > The present progressive is used because the word *now*
  > indicates that you want to know what John is studying at
  > this particular time as opposed to all other times.

• *Mary, are you working for the government?*
  ⌞___⌟

  trabajas
  present tense

  > The present tense is used because you are asking where
  > Mary is working in general over a period of time.

• *Mary, are you working right now?*
  ⌞___⌟

  estás trabajando
  present progressive

  > The present progressive is used because the words *right now*
  > indicate that you want to know if Mary is working at this
  > particular time as opposed to all other times.

Practice

The following English sentences contain the present progressive tense. Decide whether the Spanish version would use the present tense (PRES) or the present progressive (PRES PROG).

• Circle your choice

1. This semester Robert is studying physics.   PRES   PRES PROG

2. Children, why are you making so much noise?   PRES   PRES PROG

3. I can't come to the phone. I am getting ready
   to go out.   PRES   PRES PROG

4. My brother is working for a computer
   firm in California.   PRES   PRES PROG

5. My brother is doing very well.   PRES   PRES PROG

What is Meant by Mood?

Verbs are divided into "moods" which, in turn, are subdivided into one or more tenses. The word *mood* is a variation of the word *mode* meaning manner or way. The various moods indicate the attitude of the speaker toward what he or she is saying. For instance, if you are making a statement you use one mood, but if you are giving an order you use another. As a beginning student of Spanish, you only have to recognize the names of the moods so that you will know what your Spanish textbook is referring to when it uses these terms. You will learn when to use the various moods as you learn verbs and their tenses.

In English: Verbs can be in one of three moods.

1. The **indicative mood** is used to state the action of the verb, that is, to *indicate* facts. This is the most common mood, and most of the verb forms that you use in everyday conversation belong to the indicative mood. The present tense (see p. 78), the past tense (see p. 80), and the future tense (see p. 110) are all example of tenses in the indicative mood.

> Robert *studies* Spanish.
>
> present indicative

> Anita *was* here.
>
> past indicative

> They *will arrive* tomorrow.
>
> future indicative

2. The **imperative mood** is used to express the action of the verb in the form of a comand (see **What is the Imperative?**, p. 99). This mood is not divided into tenses.

> Robert, *study* Spanish now!
>
> command form of the verb

> Anita, *be* home on time!
>
> command form of the verb

3. The **subjunctive mood** is used to express an attitude or feeling toward the action of the verb. Since it stresses feelings about the fact or the idea, it is "subjective" about them. (See **What is the Subjunctive?**, p. 95.) This mood is not divided into tenses.

> The school requires that students *study* Spanish.
> I wish that Anita *were* here.
> The teacher recommends that he *do* his homework.

In Spanish: The Spanish language identifies two moods: the indicative and the subjunctive.

1. As in English, the indicative mood is the most common, and most of the tenses you will learn belong to this mood.

2. The subjunctive mood is used much more frequently in Spanish than in English. The Spanish subjunctive has four tenses: present, imperfect, present perfect, and pluperfect. In addition, most imperative or command forms are also present subjunctive forms. Textbooks will use the term "present subjunctive" to distinguish that tense from the "present indicative."

Practice

A. Fill in the blanks.

Mood is a term used in reference to (1) _____, not

nouns. The most common mood in English and in Spanish is the

(2) _____ mood. The (3) _____,

(4) _____, and (5) _____ are

examples of some of the tenses in this mood. When I order someone

to do something, I am using the (6) _____ mood.

The third mood is the (7) _____ which is used to

stress the speaker's attitude toward what he or she is saying.

B. Identify the mood of the *italicized verbs* in the following sentences.
  • Circle IND (indicative) if the verb expresses facts or SUBJ (subjunctive) if the verb stresses the speaker's attitude toward what he or she is saying.

1. We *are going* to the movies tonight.   IND   SUBJ

2. I wish we *were going* to Mexico this summer.   IND   SUBJ

3. It's important that you *do* your homework.   IND   SUBJ

4. John always *does* his homework.   IND   SUBJ

5. If I *were* you, I wouldn't do that.   IND   SUBJ

6. They *were* in Spain last week.   IND   SUBJ

What is the Subjunctive?

The **subjunctive** is a mood used to express a wish, hope, uncertainty, or other similar attitude toward a fact or an idea. Since it stresses the speaker's feelings about the fact or idea, it is usually "subjective" about them.

In English: The subjunctive is used in only a very few constructions. The subjunctive verb form is difficult to recognize because it is spelled like other tenses of the verb.

> I *am* in Detroit right now.

present indicative of *to be*

> I wish I *were* in Madrid right now.

subjunctive spelled like past tense of *to be*

He *reads* a book each week.

present indicative of *to read*

The professor insists that he *read* a book each week.

subjunctive spelled like the
dictionary form of *to read*

The subjunctive occurs most commonly in the subordinate clause of three kinds of sentences.

1. The subjunctive of the verb *to be* (*were*) is used in conditional clauses introduced by *if*.

if clause   result clause

If I *were* in Europe now, I would go to Madrid.

subjunctive

If John *were* in shape, he would run faster.

subjunctive

2. The same subjunctive form *were* is used in statements expressing a wish that is not possible.

I wish I *were* in Europe right now.

subjunctive

I wish she *were* my teacher.

subjunctive

3. The subjunctive of any verb, which is the same as the dictionary form of that verb, is used in the clause following expressions of necessity or demand, often with verbs of asking, urging, demanding, and requesting.

It is necessary that he *be* here.

subjunctive

I asked that she *come* to see me.
|
subjunctive

In Spanish: The subjunctive is used very frequently, but unfortunately English usage will rarely help you decide where or how to use it in Spanish. Therefore, we refer you to your Spanish textbook. First, learn how to conjugate regular and irregular verbs in the present subjunctive. Then, learn the verbs and expressions that require you to put the verbs that follow into the subjunctive. Learn to form and use the other subjunctive tenses in the same way.

Following are some examples of a few of the types of expressions requiring the use of a subjunctive in Spanish.

1. Verb of desire followed by a verb in the subjunctive: **querer** (*to want*)

    Quiero que Uds. **estudien** mucho.
    | |
    querer   present subjunctive
                         estudiar

    *I want you **to study** a lot.*

    (Word-for-word: I want that you *study* a lot.)

2. Expression of doubt or uncertainty followed by a verb in the subjunctive: **dudar** (*to doubt*)

    Dudo que Roberto **llegue** hoy.
    | |
    dudar   present subjunctive
                         llegar

    *I doubt that Robert **will arrive** today.*

    (Word-for-word: I doubt that Robert *arrives* today.)

3. Impersonal expression followed by a verb in the subjunctive:
   es posible (*it is possible*)

   Es posible que **compremos** un coche nuevo.
                          |
                   present subjunctive
                      comprar

   It's possible that we will buy a new car.

   (Word-for-word: It is possible that we *buy* a new car.)

4. Verb of advice or command followed by a verb in the subjunctive:
   aconsejar (*to advise*)

   Te aconsejo que **comas** muchas legumbres.
        | |
   aconsejar   present subjunctive
                     comer

   I advise you to eat a lot of vegetables.

   (Word-for-word: I advise that you *eat* a lot of vegetables.)

5. Expression of emotion followed by a verb in the subjunctive:
   sentir (*to be sorry*)

   Siento que Julio **esté** enfermo.
      | |
   sentir   present subjunctive
                   estar

   I am sorry that Julio is sick.

Practice

A. Look at the verbs in italics in the following sentences. Decide if they would be in the indicative (IND) mood or subjunctive (SUBJ) mood in Spanish.
   • Circle your choice.

1. John wants Mary *to go out* with him.   IND   SUBJ

2. I'm happy that you *got* a good job.   IND   SUBJ

3. My mother says that Tom *is* a good student. IND   SUBJ

4. The doctor suggests that you *take* two
   aspirins for your fever.   IND   SUBJ

5. It's important for you *to learn* Spanish.   IND   SUBJ

6. We doubt that he *won* the lottery.   IND   SUBJ

7. I know that John *lives* in that house.   IND   SUBJ

What is the Imperative?

The **imperative** is the command form of a verb. It is used to give someone an order. There are affirmative commands (an order to do something) and negative commands (an order not to do something).

In English: There are two types of commands.

1. The **you** command is used when giving an order to one person or many persons. The dictionary form of the verb is used for the *you* command.

   AFFIRMATIVE   NEGATIVE
   Answer the phone.   Don't *answer* the phone.
   Clean your room.   Don't *clean* your room.
   Talk softly.   Don't *talk* softly.

Notice that the pronoun "you" is not stated. The absence of the pronoun *you* in the sentence is a good indication that you are dealing with an imperative and not a present tense.

2. The **we** command is used when the speaker gives a suggestion to himself as well as others. In English this form begins with the phrase "let us" or "let's" followed by the dictionary form of the verb.

AFFIRMATIVE	NEGATIVE
Let's leave.	*Let's not leave.*
Let's go to the movies.	*Let's not go* to the movies.

In Spanish: There are also two basic types of commands: the *you command* and the *we command*. However, there are many forms of the *you command* to distinguish familiar and formal as well as affirmative and negative commands. (See **What is Meant by Familiar and Formal You?**, p. 43.)

You COMMAND

1. The **tú** command (familiar singular *you*) is used to give an order to a child, animal, or a person you know well. The affirmative **tú** command has the same form as the third-person singular of the present indicative tense. (Some verbs have irregular forms that you will have to learn individually.) The negative **tú** command has the same form as the second-person singular of the present subjunctive.

AFFIRMATIVE	NEGATIVE
Habla.	**No hables.**
Speak.	*Don't speak.*
Sal de aquí.	**No salgas** de aquí.
Leave here.	*Don't leave here.*

2. The **vosotros** command (familiar plural *you*) is used to give an order to two or more persons you know well, children, or animals. These commands are used only in Spain. The affirmative **vosotros** command is formed by dropping the "-r" from the infinitive ending and replacing it with the letter "-d." The negative **vosotros** command has the same form as the second person plural of the present subjunctive.

AFFIRMATIVE	NEGATIVE
Hablad.	**No habléis.**
Speak.	*Don't speak.*
Salid de aquí.	**No salgáis** de aquí.
Leave here.	*Don't leave here.*

3. The **usted** command (formal singular *you*) is used to give an order to a person you do not know well. Both the affirmative and negative **usted** commands have the same form as the third person singular of the present subjunctive.

AFFIRMATIVE	NEGATIVE
Hable.	**No hable.**
Speak.	*Don't speak.*
Salga de aquí.	**No salga** de aquí.
Leave here.	*Don't leave here.*

4. The **ustedes** command (in Spain: formal plural you; in Latin America: familiar and formal plural *you*) in Spain is used to give an order to more than one person that you do not know well. In Latin America the **ustedes** command is used to give an order to persons that you do or do not know well. Both the affirmative and negative **ustedes** commands have the same form as the third-person plural of the present subjunctive.

AFFIRMATIVE	NEGATIVE
Hablen.	**No hablen.**
Speak.	*Don't speak.*
Salgan de aquí.	**No salgan** de aquí.
Leave here.	*Don't leave here.*

The use of **usted** or **ustedes** following the command is option-al. It is considered somewhat more polite to use the pronoun, but is is not rude to omit it.

WE COMMAND

The affirmative and negative **nosotros** command has the same form as the first-person plural of the present subjunctive.

AFFIRMATIVE	NEGATIVE
Hablemos.	**No hablemos.**
Let's talk.	*Let's not talk.*
Salgamos.	**No salgamos.**
Let's leave.	*Let's not leave.*

Notice that the English phrase "let's" does not translate into Spanish; the command ending is the equivalent of "let's."

Here is a chart you can use as a reference for choosing the proper form of the Spanish command.

COMMAND FORM	AFFIRMATIVE	NEGATIVE
tú	Present indicative 3rd pers. sing.	Present subjunctive 2nd pers. sing.
vosotros	Infinitive -r ⟶ -d	Present subjunctive 2nd pers. pl.
usted	Present subjunctive 3rd pers. sing.	Present subjunctive 3rd pers. sing.
ustedes	Present subjunctive 3rd pers. pl.	Present subjunctive 3rd pers. pl.
nosotros	Present subjunctive 1st pers. pl.	Present subjunctive 1st pers. pl.

Practice

A. Change the following sentences to an affirmative command.

1. You should study every evening.

_____

2. We go to the movies once a week.

_____

B. Change the following sentences to a negative command.

1. You shouldn't sleep in class.

_____

2. You aren't talking a lot.

_____

C. The following are five sentences in Spanish.
- Look at the infinitive in parentheses before each sentence.
- Indicate if the verb in the sentence is a command (C) or the present tense (P). Circle the appropriate letter.

1. (estudiar) Estudien.   C   P

2. (comer) No comas más.   C   P

3. (escribir) Escriben cartas.   C   P

4. (escuchar) Escuche al profesor.   C   P

5. (bailar) Bailemos.   C   P

6. (leer) No lee mucho.   C   P

What are the Perfect Tenses?

The **perfect tenses** are compound verbs made up of the auxiliary verb *to have* + the past participle of the main verb (see **What is a Participle?**, p. 84).

I *have* not *seen* him.
     | |
auxiliary   past participle
   verb   of *to see*

They *had* already *gone*.
      | |
 auxiliary   past participle
    verb   of *to go*

The auxiliary verb *to have* can be put in different tenses. For example, *I have* is the present tense and *I have seen* is the present perfect tense. *They had* is the past tense and *they had gone* is the past perfect tense.

In English: There are four perfect tenses formed with the auxiliary verb *to have* + the past participle of the main verb. The name of each perfect tense is based on the tense used for the auxiliary verb *to have*.

1. **Present perfect:** *to have* in the present tense + the past participle of the main verb.

I *have eaten.*
  | |
auxiliary past participle
  verb   *to eat*

The boys *have washed* the car.
            | |
        auxiliary   past participle
           verb   *to wash*

2. **Past perfect** (pluperfect): *to have* in the simple past + the past participle of the main verb. (See **What is the Past Tense?**, p. 80.)

> I *had eaten* before 6:00.
> auxiliary   past participle
>   verb   *to eat*

> The boys *had washed* the car before the storm.
>   auxiliary   past participle
>   verb   *to wash*

3. **Future perfect**: *to have* in the future tense + the past participle of the main verb. (See **What is the Future Tense?**, p. 110.)

> I *will have eaten* by 6:00.
>   auxiliary   past participle
>   verbs   *to eat*

> The boys *will have washed* the car by Thursday.
>   auxiliary   past participle
>   verbs   *to wash*

4. **Conditional perfect**: *to have* in the conditional + the past participle of the main verb. (See **What is the Conditional?**, p. 114.)

> I *would have eaten* if I had had the time.
>   auxiliary   past participle
>   verbs   *to eat*

> The boys *would have washed* the car if they had been
> here.   auxiliary   past participle
>   verbs   *to wash*

In Spanish: The perfect tenses are made up of a form of the auxiliary verb **haber** + the past participle of the main verb. In Spanish there are several perfect tenses: four perfect tenses in the indicative and two in the subjunctive. As in English, the name of the tense is based on the tense of the auxiliary verb **haber**. (See **What is the Subjunctive?**, p. 95.)

We are listing the various perfect tenses here so that you can see the pattern that they follow. You will see that an entire section is devoted to the perfect tenses that do not function the same in both Spanish and English.

PERFECT TENSES IN THE INDICATIVE MOOD

1. **Present perfect** (perfecto): **haber** in the present tense + the past participle of the main verb.

> **He comido.**
> *I have eaten.*

> Los chicos **han lavado** el coche.
> *The boys **have washed** the car.*

Generally the Spanish present perfect is used in the same way as the present perfect in English.

2. **Pluperfect or past perfect** (pluscuamperfecto): **haber** in the imperfect + the past participle of the main verb. The pluperfect tense is used to express an action completed in the past before some other past action or event.

> **Había comido** antes de las seis.
> *I had eaten before 6:00.*

> Los chicos **habían lavado** el coche antes de la tempestad.
> *The boys **had washed** the car before the storm.*

Generally, the Spanish past perfect is used the same way as the past perfect in English.

3. **Future perfect** (futuro perfecto): **haber** in the future + the past participle of the main verb. (See **What is the Future Tense?**, p. 110.)

> **Habré comido** para las seis.
> *I will have eaten by 6:00.*

> Los chicos **habrán lavado** el coche para el jueves.
> *The boys will have washed the car by Thursday.*

Generally, the Spanish future perfect is used in the same way as the future perfect in English.

4. **Conditional perfect** (condicional perfecto): **haber** in the conditional + the past participle of the main verb. (See **What is the Conditional?**, p. 114.)

> **Habría comido** si hubiera tenido el tiempo.
> *I would have eaten if I had had the time.*

> Los chicos **habrían lavado** el coche si hubieran estado aquí.
> *The boys would have washed the car if they had been here.*

PERFECT TENSES IN THE SUBJUNCTIVE MOOD (See **What is the Subjunctive?**, p. 95.)

1. **Present perfect subjunctive** (Perfecto del subjuntivo): **haber** in the present subjunctive + the past participle of the main verb. This tense is really just a present perfect used when a subjunctive is required.

*He knows that they **have arrived**.*

han llegado
present perfect

*He hopes that they **have arrived**.*

hayan llegado
present perfect

A subjunctive is used because *hopes* (the verb in the main clause) requires a subjunctive in the dependent clause.

2. **Pluperfect subjunctive** (pluscuamperfecto del subjuntivo): **haber** in the imperfect subjunctive + the past participle of the main verb.

*He knew that they **had arrived**.*

habían llegado
pluperfect tense

*He hoped that they **had arrived**.*

hubieran llegado
pluperfect subjunctive

A subjunctive is needed because *hoped* (the verb in the main clause) requires a subjunctive in the dependent clause.

Practice

A. Fill in the blanks.

In English the perfect tenses are formed with the auxiliary verb

(1) _____ followed by the (2) _____.

In English there are (3) _____ perfect tenses. In

Spanish there are (4) _____ perfect tenses in the

indicative mood and (5) _____ in the subjunctive

mood. The name of the perfect tense is based on the tense of the

(6) _____.

B. The following sentences all have verbs in a perfect tense.
  • Underline the verbs in a perfect tense.
  • Write out the complete English name of that verb tense on the line
    provided below each sentence.

1. We had already gone when Teresa arrived.

   _____

2. Barbara hasn't left yet.

   _____

3. I will have graduated by next summer.

   _____

4. We would have studied more if we had remembered the exam.

_____

5. Have you seen my new car?

_____

What is the Future Tense?

The **future tense** indicates that an action will take place some time in the future.

In English: The future tense is formed with the auxiliary *will* or *shall* + the dictionary form of the main verb. Note that *shall* is used in very formal English (and British English); *will* occurs in everyday language.

> I *will leave* tonight.
> Paul and Mary *will do* their homework tomorrow.

In conversation *will* is often shortened to *'ll* and *will not* is often shortened to *won't*.

> I'*ll* leave tomorrow.
> Paul and Mary *won't* do their homework tonight.

In Spanish: You do not need an auxiliary verb to show that an action will take place. Future time is indicated by a simple tense.

Most verbs use the infinitive as a stem for the future tense.

INFINITIVE	STEM	
visitar	visitar-	*to visit*
comer	comer-	*to eat*
vivir	vivir-	*to live*

A few verbs such as those in the following list, have irregular future stems that must be memorized.

INFINITIVE	STEM	
venir	vendr -	*to come*
decir	dir-	*to say, tell*
saber	sabr-	*to know*

Your textbook will show you how to conjugate regular and irregular verbs in the future tense.

SUBSTITUTES FOR THE FUTURE TENSE

In English and in Spanish the fact that an action will occur some time in the future can also be expressed without using the future tense itself but rather a structure that implies the future.

In English: You can use the verb *to go* in the present progressive + the dictionary form of the main verb: *I am going to travel, she is going to dance.*

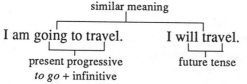

In Spanish: The same construction exists in Spanish. You can use the verb **ir** (*to go*) in the present tense + **a** + the infinitive.

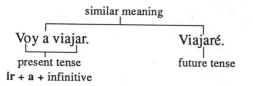

Note that the "a" has no English equivalent; it must appear in the Spanish sentence, however.

In conversational Spanish **ir a** + infinitive often replaces the future tense.

Sometimes the present tense is used to express a future idea especially when discussing a future event that is pre-arranged and certain to happen.

Mañana **tienen** un examen.
present tense

*Tomorrow you **will have** an exam.*
future tense

FUTURE OF PROBABILITY

In addition to expressing an action which will take place in the future, in Spanish the future tense can be used to express a probable fact, what the speaker feels is probably true. This is called the **future of probability.**

In English: The idea of probability is expressed with words such as *must, probably, wonder.*

My keys *must* be around here.
My keys are *probably* around here.
I *wonder* if my keys are around here.

In Spanish: It is not necessary to use the words *must, probably,* or *wonder* to express probable facts; the main verb is simply put into the future tense.

*I wonder what time it **is**.*
present tense   main verb

¿Qué hora **será**?
future tense
main verb

It's probably 4:00.
|
main verb *is*
present tense

Serán las cuatro.
|
main verb
future tense

I can't find my book. Juan must have it.
|
main verb
present tense

No puedo encontrar mi libro. Juan lo **tendrá.**
|
main verb
future tense

Practice

A. The following are sentences with verbs in the future tense.
- Circle the verbs.
- On the line provided, write the dictionary form of the English verb you would put in the future tense in Spanish.

DICTIONARY FORM

1. The students will study for the exam. _____

2. I'll clean my room later. _____

3. Shall we leave? _____

4. I won't finish until tomorrow. _____

5. Will she be here by 9:00? _____

B. The following sentences all express probable facts.
   • Circle the expression of probability.
   • On the line provided, write the dictionary form of the English verb you would put in the future tense in Spanish.

                                                        DICTIONARY FORM

1. I wonder who is at the door.   _____

2. It's probably my mother.   _____

3. Who might have my Spanish book?   _____

4. Debbie must have it.   _____

5. Mr. Jones is probably going to win the   _____
   election.

What is the Conditional?

The conditional does not exist as a separate tense in English and some modern English grammar books do not include it. However, the conditional is a very important tense in Spanish. There is an English verb form which is similar to the Spanish conditional and which can help you understand it. For our purposes, we will call this form the "conditional."

In English: The "conditional" has a present and past tense called the **conditional** (present) and the **conditional perfect** (past).

A. CONDITIONAL

The conditional is a compound tense. It is formed with the auxiliary *would* + the dictionary form of the main verb.

> I said that I *would come* tomorrow.
> If she had the money, she *would call* him.
> I *would like* some ketchup, please.

NOTE: The auxiliary *would* in English has several meanings. It does not correspond to the conditional when it stands for *used to*, as in "She *would* talk while he painted." In this sentence, the verb "would talk" means *used to talk* and requires the imperfect of the verb *to talk* in Spanish (see p. 81).

The conditional is used in the following ways:

1. in the main clause of a hypothetical statement

> If I had a lot of money, I *would buy* a Cadillac.

"I would buy a Cadillac" is called the **main clause**, or **result clause**. It is a clause because it is composed of a group of words containing a subject (*I*) and a verb (*would buy*) and is used as part of sentence. It is the main clause because it expresses a complete thought and can stand by itself without being attached to the first part of the sentence ("If I had a lot of money"). It is called the result clause because it expresses what would happen as the result of getting a lot of money.

"If I had a lot of money" is called the **subordinate clause**, or **if-clause**. It is called subordinate because, although it contains a subject (*I*) and a verb (*had*), it does not express a complete thought and cannot stand alone. It must be attached to the main clause.

The entire statement is called **hypothetical** because it refers to a condition that does not exist at the present time (the person speaking does not have a lot of money), but there may be a remote possibility of its becoming a reality (the person speaking could have a lot of money some day).

2. in an indirect statement to express a future-in-the-past

> He said Mary *would come*.
>   (1)   (2)

"He said" is the main clause. The verb "said" prepares you for either a word-for-word quotation, called **direct speech**, or a summary of what was said, called **indirect speech**. "Mary would come" is an indirect statement (it summarized what he said).

Action (1) is in the past and action (2) is to take place after Action (1), but still in the past. Action (2) is called a **future-in-the-past** because it takes place after another action in the past.

3. as a polite form with *like* and in polite requests

> I *would like* to eat.
>
> > This is more polite than "I want to eat."

> *Would* you please close the door.
>
> > The command "please close the door"
> > is softened by the use of *would*.

B. CONDITIONAL PERFECT

The **conditional perfect** is formed with the auxiliary *would have* + the past participle of the main verb.

Unlike some statements in the conditional where there is a possibility of their becoming a reality, all statements using the conditional perfect are contrary-to-fact: the main action never happened because the condition expressed was never met and it is now over and done with.

He *would have spoken* if he had known the truth.

> Contrary-to-fact: He did not speak because he did not know the truth.

If you had called us, we *would have come.*

> Contrary-to-fact: We did not come because you didn't call us.

I *would have eaten* if I had been hungry.

> Contrary-to-fact: I did not eat because I wan't hungry.

In Spanish: The conditional is a simple tense; you do not need an auxiliary verb to indicate it. The conditional is formed with the future stem (see p. 110) + the endings of the imperfect tense for -er and -ir verbs (-ía, -ías, -ía, -íamos, -íais, -ían).

STEM	CONDITIONAL	
hablar-	hablaría	*I would speak*
comer-	comería	*I would eat*
vivir-	viviría	*I would live*
pondr-	pondría	*I would put*
har-	haría	*I would do*

The conditional is used in the following ways:

1. in the main clause of a hypothetical statement to express what you would do under certain conditions

> Si tuviera mucho dinero, **compraría** una casa grande.
> |
> conditional

*If I had a lot of money, I **would buy** a big house.*

2. in an indirect statement to express a future-in-the-past

> Dijo que **vendría.**
> |
> conditional

> *He said that he **would come.***

> Sabía que **llovería** esta noche.
> |
> conditional

> *I knew that it **would rain** this evening.*

3. as a polite form or in polite requests

> ¿**Podría** Ud. cerrar la puerta, por favor?
> |
> conditional

> ***Could** you close the door, please?*

B. CONDITIONAL PERFECT

The conditional perfect is formed with the auxiliary verb **haber** in the conditional tense + the past participle of the main verb: **habría salido** (see p. 86). As in English, statements using the conditional perfect are contrary-to-fact.

> Si hubieran estudiado más, **habrían recibido** mejores
> notas.   conditional perfect

> *If they had studied more, they **would have received** better grades.*

SEQUENCE OF TENSES

Let us study some examples of constructions with conditions and their results so that you learn to recognize them and to use the appropriate Spanish tense.

Hypothetical and contrary-to-fact statements are easy to recognize because they are made up of two clauses:

*   the if-clause; that is, the subordinate clause that starts with *if* (si in Spanish)

*   the result clause; that is, the main clause

The sequence of tenses is sometimes the same in both Spanish and English. If you have difficulty recognizing tenses, just apply these three rules.

*   if-clause = present tense
    result clause = future tense

> *If I have time, I will go to the party.*
> | |
>   present   future

> Si **tengo** tiempo, **iré** a la fiesta.
> | |
>   present   future

*   if-clause = past tense in English
                     imperfect subjunctive in Spanish
    result clause = conditional

> *If I had more time, I would go to the party.*
> | |
>   past   conditional

> Si **tuviera** más tiempo, **iría** a la fiesta.
> | |
>   imperfect   conditional
>   subjunctive

- if clause = past perfect in English
            pluperfect subjunctive in Spanish
  result clause = conditional perfect

*If I **had had** more time, I **would have gone** to the party.*
            | |
      past perfect   conditional perfect

Si **hubiera tenido** más tiempo, **habría ido** a la fiesta.
        | |
  pluperfect subjunctive   conditional perfect

In English and in Spanish the if-clause can come either at the beginning of the sentence before the main clause or at the end of the sentence. The tense of each clause remains the same no matter the order of the clauses.

Practice

Some of the verbs in the following sentences are in *italics*.
- For each of the verbs in italics, identify the tense you would use in Spanish by writing the name of the tense on the line provided: present, future, conditional, conditional perfect, imperfect subjunctive, pluperfect subjunctive or the imperfect.

1. I know the children *would enjoy* that movie.   _____

2. We *would go* to Spain if we *had* the money.   _____

    _____

3. I *would like* some more meat, please.   _____

4. If it *rains*, they *won't have* the picnic.   _____

5. My parents wrote that they *would come* in July.   _____

6. If I *had known* you were coming, I *wouldn't have left.* _____

_____

7. When he was little, he *would play* baseball a lot. _____

What is a Reflexive Verb?

A **reflexive verb** is a verb that is linked to a special pronoun called a **reflexive pronoun**; this pronoun serves to *reflect* the action of the verb back to the performer, that is, to the subject of the sentence. The result is that the subject of the sentence and the object are the same person.

> *She* cut *herself* with the knife.
> *He* saw *himself* in the mirror.

In English: Many verbs can take on a reflexive meaning by adding a reflexive pronoun.

> Peter *cut* the paper.
> |
>   regular verb

> Peter *cut himself* when he shaved.
> |
>   verb + reflexive pronoun

Pronouns ending with *-self* or *-selves* are used to make verbs reflexive. Here are the reflexive pronouns.

	SUBJECT PRONOUN	REFLEXIVE PRONOUN
SINGULAR	I	myself
	you	yourself
	he	himself
	she	herself
	it	itself
PLURAL	we	ourselves
	you	yourselves
	they	themselves

In a sentence a reflexive pronoun is always tied to a specific subject, because both the pronoun and the subject refer to the same person or object.

> *I* cut *myself.*
> *Paul and Mary* blamed *themselves* for the accident.

Although the subject pronoun *you* is the same for the singular and plural, there is a difference between the reflexive pronouns used: *yourself* is used when you are speaking to one person (singular) and *yourselves* is used when you are speaking to more than one (plural).

> Paul, did you make *yourself* a sandwich?
> Children, make sure you dry *yourselves* properly.

In Spanish: As in English many regular verbs can be turned into reflexive verbs by adding a reflexive pronoun.

> Roberto **lava** el coche.
> *Robert washes the car.*

> Roberto **se lava.**
> *Robert washes himself.*

The dictionary lists **lavar** as the infinitive of **to wash** and **lavarse** as the infinitive of *to wash oneself.*

Here are the Spanish reflexive pronouns:

me	*myself*
te	*yourself* (fam. sing.)
se	*himself, herself, yourself* (form. sing.)
nos	*ourselves*
os	*yourselves* (fam. pl.)
se	*themselves, yourselves* (pl. form and fam.)

Since the reflexive pronoun reflects the action of the verb back to the performer, the reflexive pronoun will change as the subject of the verb changes. You will have to memorize the conjugation of the reflexive verbs with the subject pronoun and the reflexive pronoun. For example, let's look at the conjugation of **lavarse** in the present tense. Notice that, unlike English, where the reflexive pronoun is placed after the verb, in Spanish the reflexive pronoun is placed immediately before the verb.

SUBJECT PRONOUN	REFLEXIVE PRONOUN	VERB
yo	me	lavo
tú	te	lavas
él ella Ud.	se	lava
nosotros nosotras	nos	lavamos
vosotros vosotras	os	laváis
ellos ellas Uds.	se	lavan

Reflexive verbs can be conjugated in all tenses. The subject pronoun and the reflexive pronoun remain the same, regardless of the tense of the verb: **él se lavará** (future); **ellos se lavaron** (preterite).

USE OF REFLEXIVE VERBS

Reflexive verbs are more common in Spanish than in English; that is, there are many verbs that take a reflexive pronoun in Spanish but not in English. For example, when you say, "Mary washed in the morning," it is understood, but not stated, that "Mary washed herself." In Spanish the "herself" must be stated: "María se lavó." In addition, other English verbs such as *to get up* have a reflexive meaning. "Mary got up" means that she got herself up. In Spanish you express *to get up* by using the verb **levantarse,** that is **levantar** (*to raise*) + the reflexive pronoun se (*oneself*): "María se levantó." You must memorize the many verbs that require a reflexive pronoun in Spanish.

Practice

A. Fill in the proper reflexive pronoun.

1. The children wash _____ every evening.

2. Mary always blames _____.

3. Mary, you always blame _____.

4. Children, behave _____.

5. They do everything to suit _____.

B. Complete the following list of subject pronouns by writing the corresponding reflexive pronouns in the spaces provided.

SUBJECT   REFLEXIVE
PRONOUN   PRONOUN

1. Uds.   _____

2. Carlos y yo   _____

2. tú   _____

4 Juan   _____

5. yo   _____

6. María y Susana   _____

What is Meant by Active and Passive Voice?

The voice of the verb refers to a basic relationship between the verb and its subject. There are two voices:

The **active voice** —A sentence is said to be in the active voice when the subject is the performer of the verb. In this instance, the verb is called an **active verb**.

The teacher writes the exam.
    S   V   DO

Paul ate an apple.
 S V   DO

Lightning has struck the tree.
    S   V   DO

In all these examples, the subject (s) performs the action of the verb (v) and the direct object (DO) is the receiver of the action.

The **passive voice** —A sentence is said to be in the passive voice when the subject is the receiver of the action. In this instance, the verb is called a **passive verb**.

> The exam is written by the teacher.
>   S   V   Agent

> The apple was eaten by Paul.
>   S   V   Agent

> The tree has been struck by lightning.
>   S   V   Agent

In all these examples, the subject is having the action of the verb performed upon it. The performer of the action, if it is mentioned, is introduced by the word *by*. It is called the **agent**.

In English: The passive voice is expressed by the verb *to be* conjugated in the appropriate tense + the past participle of the main verb. The tense of the passive sentence is indicated by the tense of the verb *to be*.

> The exam *is written* by the teacher.
>   present

> The exam *was written* by the teacher.
>   past

> The exam *will be written* by the teacher.
>   future

ACTIVE SENTENCE ⟶ PASSIVE SENTENCE

When an active sentence is changed into a passive sentence the following changes occur:

1. The direct object of the active sentence becomes the subject of the passive sentence.

    ACTIVE: The teacher writes *the exam.*
                                  direct object

    PASSIVE: *The exam* is written by the teacher.
                    subject

2. The tense of the verb of the active sentence is reflected in the tense of the verb *to be* in the passive sentence.

    ACTIVE   The teacher *writes* the exam.
                         present

    PASSIVE   The exam *is* written by the teacher.
                     present

    ACTIVE   The teacher *wrote* the exam.
                         past

    PASSIVE   The exam *was* written by the teacher.
                     past

    ACTIVE   The teacher *will* write the exam.
                      future

    PASSIVE   The exam *will be* written by the teacher.
                       future

3. The subject of the active sentence becomes the agent of the passive sentence introduced with *by*. The agent is often omitted.

ACTIVE   The *teacher* writes the exam.
                                    |
                                 subject

PASSIVE   The exam is written by the *teacher*.
                                                        |
                                                     agent

In Spanish: As in English, a passive verb can be expressed by the auxiliary verb **ser** (*to be*) conjugated in the appropriate tense + the past participle of the main verb. The tense of the passive sentence is indicated by the tense of the verb **ser**.

El examen **es** escrito por el profesor.
          |
       present

The exam is written by the teacher.

El examen **fue** escrito por el profesor.
          |
       preterite

The exam was written by the teacher.

El examen **será** escrito por el profesor.
          |
       future

The exam will be written by the teacher.

PAST PASSIVE OR PAST PERFECT

Be careful not to confuse a passive sentence in the past tense with an active sentence in the present perfect. For instance, **ha cerrado** is the present perfect of the verb **cerrar** (*to close*) and **fue cerrado** is the past passive. As you can see in the following examples, the same changes occur in English.

ACTIVE   *The teacher has written the exam.*

                              |
                      present perfect

PASSIVE   *The exam was written by the teacher.*

                              |
                      past passive

ACTIVE   El profesor **ha escrito** el examen.

                              |
                      present perfect

PASSIVE   El examen **fue escrito** por el profesor.

                              |
                      past passive

Because the auxiliary verb in the passive voice is always **ser**, all past participles agree in gender and number with the subject.

Esas **cartas** fueron **escritas** por el profesor.

        | |
    fem. pl.   fem. pl.

*Those **letters** were **written** by the teacher.*

AVOIDING THE PASSIVE

Although Spanish has a passive voice, it does not favor its use as English does, and whenever possible Spanish speakers try to avoid the passive construction by replacing it with an active one. This is particulary true for general statements of the following kind.

English is spoken in many countries.
The office opens at 9:00.

There are two ways a passive sentence can be avoided.

1. by using the **se** construction

The word **se** corresponds to the English *one, they, you,* or *it* used in a general sense as in "One should eat when one is hungry" or "They say he's a nice guy."

In order to use the **se** construction as a replacement for the passive voice

    a. transform the English passive sentence to an active sentence using *one* as the subject

        English *is spoken* in many countries.
        One speaks English in many countries.

        The office *opens* at 9:00.
        One opens the office at 9:00.

    b.   transform the active sentence into Spanish

        One speaks English in many countries.
        Se habla inglés en muchos países.

        One opens the office at 9:00.
        Se abre la oficina a las nueve.

2. by using the third person plural of the verb

To avoid the passive construction Spanish often makes *they* (the third person plural) the subject of an active sentence. The "they" corresponds to a general subject such as "They say Mexico is very interesting."

In order to use the third person plural as a replacement for the passive voice

    a. transform the English passive sentence to an active sentence using *they* as a subject

        English is spoken in many countries.
        They speak English in many countries.

        The office opens at 9:00.
        They open the office at 9:00.

b. transform the active sentence into Spanish

They speak English in many countries.
Hablan inglés en muchos países.

They open the office at 9:00.
Abren la oficina a las nueve.

Practice

A. In the following sentences:
- Underline the subject of the sentence.
- Circle the performer of the action.
- Identify each sentence by writing "A" for active or "P" for passive on the line provided.

1. The cow jumped over the moon.   _____

2. The bill was paid by Bob's parents.   _____

3. The bank transfers the money.   _____

4. Everyone will be going away during August._____

5. The spring break will be enjoyed by all.   _____

B. The following sentences are in the active voice.
  • Underline the verb.
  • Identify the tense of the verb by writing the appropriate letter on the line at the end of the sentence: Past (PP), Present (P), Future (F).
  • Write the sentence in the passive voice on the line below.

1. All the students are taking the final exam.

_____

2. The teacher brought the children to the park.

_____

3. People all over the world will read the article.

_____

What is an Adjective?

An **adjective** is a word that describes a noun or a pronoun.

In English: Adjectives are classified according to the way they describe a noun or pronoun.

A **descriptive adjective** indicates a quality; it describes what the noun or pronoun is like. See p. 134.

> She read an *interesting* book.
> He has *brown* eyes.

A **possessive adjective** shows possession; it explains to whom something or someone belongs. See p. 138.

His book is lost.
Our parents are away.

An **interrogative adjective** asks a question about someone or something. See p. 148.

What book is lost?
Which parents did you speak to?

A **demonstrative adjective** points out someone or something. See p. 151.

This teacher is excellent.
That question is very appropriate.

In all these cases it is said that the adjective modifies the noun or pronoun.

In Spanish: Adjectives are classified in the same way as in English. The principal difference between English and Spanish adjectives is that in English adjectives do not change their form, while in Spanish adjectives agree in gender and number with the noun or pronoun they modify.

Practice

Fill in the blanks.

An adjective is a word that describes a (1) _____ or a

(2) _____, not a verb. An adjective that describes is

called a (3) _____ adjective. An adjective that tells

you to whom something belongs is called a (4) _____.

An adjective that asks a question about someone or something is called

an (5) _____ and an adjective that points out someone

or something, is called a (6) _____ adjective. The

principal difference between English and Spanish adjectives is that

Spanish adjectives agree in (7) _____ and

(8) _____ with the word they modify while English

adjectives do not.

What is a Descriptive Adjective?

A **descriptive adjective** is a word that indicates a quality of a noun or pronoun. As the name implies, it *describes* the noun or pronoun.

In English: The descriptive adjective does not change form, regardless of the noun or pronoun it modifies.

> Mary bought an *interesting* book.
> |
>   singular noun described

> Mary bought *interesting* books.
> |
>   plural noun described

The adjective *interesting* is the same although in one instance it modifies a singular noun and in other a plural noun.

Descriptive adjectives are divided into two groups depending on how they are connected to the noun they modify.

1. An **attributive adjective** is connected directly to its noun and always precedes it.

> The *good* children were praised.
> |
> noun described

> The family lives in a *small* house.
> |
> noun described.

2. A **predicate adjective** is connected to its noun (the subject of the sentence) by a linking verb, usually a form of *to be*.

> The children are *good*.
> | | |
> noun linking predicate adjective
> subject verb

> The house looks *small*.
> | | |
> noun linking predicate adjective
> subject verb

NOUNS USED AS ADJECTIVES

You should also be able to recognize **nouns used as adjectives**; that is, a noun used to modify another noun.

> Spanish is easy.   The *Spanish* class is crowded.
> | |
>   noun   adjective

> Chemistry is difficult. The *chemistry* books are expensive.
> | |
>   noun   adjective

In Spanish: The most important difference between descriptive adjectives in Spanish and English is that in Spanish they change forms. In Spanish, an adjective, predicate and attributive, must always agree with the noun or pronoun it modifies; that is, it must correspond in gender and number to its noun. Thus, before writing an adjective, you will have to determine if the noun or pronoun it modifies is masculine or feminine, singular or plural.

Most adjectives change the final -o of the masculine singular form to -a to make the feminine form and add -s to the feminine or masculine singular form to make it plural.

<table>
<tr><td>*the red car*</td><td>el coche **rojo**
masc.   masc.
sing.   sing.</td></tr>
<tr><td>*the red table*</td><td>la mesa **roja**
fem.   fem.
sing.   sing.</td></tr>
<tr><td>*the red cars*</td><td>los coches **rojos**
masc.   masc.
pl.   pl.</td></tr>
<tr><td>*the red tables*</td><td>las mesas **rojas**
fem.   fem.
pl.   pl.</td></tr>
</table>

NOUNS USED AS ADJECTIVES

When a noun is used as an adjective, that is, to describe another noun, it remains a noun and does not change its form. Notice that a noun used as an adjective is introduced by the word **de**.

<table>
<tr><td>*the **Spanish** class*   =
el español   la clase</td><td>la **clase** de **español**
fem.   masc.
sing.   sing.</td></tr>
</table>

Word-for-word: the class of Spanish

<table>
<tr><td>*the **chemistry** books*   =
la química   los libros</td><td>los **libros** de **química**
masc.   fem.
pl.   sing.</td></tr>
</table>

Word-for-word: the books of chemistry

Practice

A. In the following sentences:
   • Circle the adjectives.
   • Draw an arrow from the adjective you circled to the noun or pronoun described.

1. The young man was reading a Spanish newspaper.

2. She looked pretty in her red dress.

3. It is interesting.

4. The old piano could still produce good music.

5. Paul was tired after his long walk.

B. The following sentences contain nouns used as adjectives.
   • Rewrite the italicized words in English so the new phrase is a word-for-word equivalent of the Spanish structure.

1. Robert just bought *a leather jacket.*

_____

2. Where is *my history notebook?*

_____

3. I need a new pair of *tennis shoes.*

_____

4. Our daughter loves *chocolate cake.*

_____

5. Do you like *tomato juice?*

_____

6. They are building a *brick house.*

_____

What is a Possessive Adjective?

A **possessive adjective** is a word that describes a noun by showing who "possesses" the thing or person being discussed. The owner is called the "possessor" and the noun modified is called the person or thing "possessed."

In English: Here is a list of the possessive adjectives:

SINGULAR	
1st PERSON	my
2nd PERSON	your
3rd PERSON	his
	her
	its
PLURAL	
1st PERSON	our
2nd PERSON	your
3rd PERSON	their

The possessive adjective refers only to the possessor and it does not agree in gender or number with the noun it modifies.

Paul's mother is young.   *His* mother is young.

possessor   person possessed

Mary's father is poor.   *Her* father is poor.
The cat's ears are short.   *Its* ears are short.

In Spanish: Unlike English where possessive adjectives refer only to the possessor, Spanish possessive adjectives refer to both the possessor and the possessed. Like all adjectives in Spanish, the possessive adjective must agree in gender and number with the noun it modifies, that is, the person or object possessed.

For example, in the phrase **nuestro hermano** (*our brother*) the first letters of the possessive adjective **nuestr-** refer to the first person plural possessor *our*, while the ending **-o** is masculine singular to agree with **hermano** which is also masculine singular. Let us see what happens when we make the noun *brother* plural.

> *We love **our brothers**.*
> Queremos a nuestros hermanos.
>   masc. pl. endings
> 1st pers. pl. possessor

Nuestros refers to the possessor (*we, our*), but agrees in gender and number with the noun **hermanos.**

Here are the steps you should follow in choosing the correct possessive adjective.

A. MY, YOUR (fam. sing.) HIS, HER, YOUR (form. sing.), THEIR, and YOUR (form. pl.)

These possessive adjectives have only two forms: singular and plural; they change only in number to agree with the noun possessed.

1. Indicate the possessor. This is shown by the two letters of the possessive adjective.

my	mi
your (fam. sing.)	tu

his	
her	
your (form. sing.)	su
their	
your (form. pl.)	

2. Make the possessive adjective agree with the noun possessed.

If the noun is singular, the form of the possessive adjective does not change.

Ana lee **mi** libro.	*Ana reads **my** book.*
Ana lee **tu** libro.	*Ana reads **your** book.*
Ana lee **su** libro.	*Ana reads **his/her/your/** *** their** book.*

If the noun is plural, add -**s** to the possessive adjective.

Ana lee **mis** libros.	*Ana reads **my** books.*
Ana lee **tus** libros.	*Ana reads **your** books.*
Ana lee **sus** libros.	*Ana reads **his/her/your/** *** their** books.*

Since the word **su** has many possible English meanings, Spanish speakers often substitute the phrase noun + **de** + prepositional pronoun for the possessive **su** in order to make the meaning clearer.

his book	el libro **de él**
her book	el libro **de ella**
your (form. sing.) *book*	el libro **de Ud.**
their book	el libro **de ellos/ellas**
your (form. pl.) *book*	el libro **de Uds.**

B. OUR, YOUR (fam. pl.)

These possessive adjectives have four forms; they change to agree in number and gender with the noun modified.

1. Indicate the possessor. This is shown by the first letters of the possessive adjective.

> *our*   nuestr-
> *your* (fam. pl.)   vuestr-

2. Fill in the possessive adjective to agree with the item possessed.

If the noun possessed is masculine singular, add **-o.**

> Ana lee **nuestro** libro.   *Ana reads **our** book.*
> masc. sing.

> Ana lee **vuestro** libro.   *Ana reads **your** book.*

If the noun possessed is feminine singular, add **-a.**

> Ana lee **nuestra** revista.   *Ana reads **our** magazine.*
> fem. sing.

> Ana lee **vuestra** revista.   *Ana reads **your** magazine.*

If the noun possessed is masculine plural, add **-os.**

> Ana lee **nuestros** libros.   *Ana reads **our** books.*
> masc. pl.

> Ana lee **vuestros** libros.   *Ana reads **your** books.*

If the noun possessed is feminine plural, add **-as.**

> Ana lee **nuestras** revistas. *Ana reads **our** magazines.*
> fem. pl.

> Ana lee **vuestras** revistas. *Ana reads **your** magazines.*

Before you write a sentence with *your*, decide whether it is appropriate to use the familiar or formal forms in Spanish. Then, make sure that every word that refers to "you" is in the appropriate form, including the verb.

Tú lees **tu** carta.
Ud. lee **su** carta.
Vosotros leéis **vuestra** carta.   } *You are reading your letter.*
Uds. leen **su** carta.

NOTE: In Spanish and in English, the subject and the possessive adjective do not necessarily match. It all depends on what you want to say.

¿Tienes **tu** libro?   *Do you have your book?*
2nd pers. sing.   2nd pers. sing.

¿Tienes **mi** libro?   *Do you have my book?*
2nd pers.   1st pers.   2nd pers.   1st pers.
sing.   sing.   sing.   sing.

STRESSED POSSESSIVE ADJECTIVES

Spanish also has another set of possessive adjectives called **stressed possessive adjectives**; they follow the noun they modify. They are used to add emphasis to the possessor and correspond to the English "of mine," "of yours," etc.: "That dress *of mine*" (instead of *my* dress); "Those books *of yours*" (instead of *your* books). The use of these stressed forms is more common in Spanish than in English.

Like the unstressed possessives the first letters of the stressed possessive adjective refers to the possessor and the ending agrees with the item or person possessed. For example, in the phrase **el libro tuyo** (*your book*) the first letters of the possessive adjective **tuy-** refer to a 2nd person singular possessor *your*; the ending -o is masculine singular to agree with **libro** which is masculine singular.

Here is a list of the stressed possessive adjectives used with a masculine singular noun.

mío	*mine; of mine*
tuyo	*your; of yours*
suyo	*his, her, your; of his, of hers,*
	of yours
nuestro	*our; of ours*
vuestro	*your; of yours*
suyo	*their, your; of theirs, of yours*

Here are the steps you should follow in choosing the correct stressed possessive adjective.

1. Indicate the possessor. This is shown by the first letters of the possessive adjective.

mine, of mine	**mí-**
your, of yours (fam. sing.)	**tuy-**
his, of his	
her, of hers	**suy-**
your, of yours (form. sing.)	
our, of ours	**nuestr-**
your, of yours (fam. pl.)	**vuestr-**
their, of theirs	**suy-**
your, of yours (form. pl.)	

2. Fill out the adjective so that it agrees in gender and number with the noun possessed. Place the stressed possessive adjective after the noun.

If the noun possessed is masculine singular, add -o.

Ana lee un libro mío.

  masc. sing.

Ana is reading a book of mine.

If the noun possessed is feminine singular, add -a.

Ana lee una revista mía.
        └──┬──┘
         fem. sing.

*Ana is reading a magazine **of mine.***

If the noun possessed is masculine plural, add -os.

Ana lee unos libros míos.
         └──┬──┘
          masc. pl.

*Ana is reading some books **of mine.***

If the noun possessed is feminine plural, add -as.

*Ana is reading some magazines **of mine.***
Ana lee unas revistas mías.
        └──┬──┘
         fem. pl.

*This car is John's. **My** car is in the garage.*

   1. Possessor: 1st person singular
   2. Gender and number of noun possessed:
      El coche (*car*) is masculine singular.

El coche mío está en el garaje.
   └──┬──┘
    masc. sing.

*These chairs **of yours** are very comfortable.*

   1. Possessor: 2nd person singular
   2. Gender and number of noun possessed:
      Las sillas (*chairs*) are feminine plural.

Estas sillas tuyas son muy cómodas.
           └──┬──┘
            fem. pl.

Practice

A. These are the steps to follow in order to choose the correct form of the Spanish possessive adjectives.
   • Fill in the missing elements in the blanks provided.

1. *My, your* (fam. sing.) *his, her, your* (form. sing.), *their,* and *your* (form. pl.)

   Indicate the _____.

   my = _____

   your (fam. sing.) = _____

   his, her, your (form. sing.) = _____

   their, your (form. pl.) = _____

   Analyze the _____ of the noun possessed.

   If the noun possessed is _____,

   the possessive adjective does not change forms.

   If the noun possessed is _____,

   add -_____.

2. *Our, your* (fam. pl.)

   Indicate the _____.

   our = _____

   your (fam. pl.) = _____

Determine the _____

and _____ of the noun possessed.

Fill in the possessive adjective.

    Add - _____ if the noun possessed is masculine singular.

    Add - _____ if the noun possessed is feminine singular.

    Add - _____ if the noun possessed is masculine plural.

    Add - _____ if the noun possessed is feminine plural.

B. Complete the steps to determine the correct form of the Spanish possessive adjectives. (Use the short, unstressed forms.)

1. Teresa lost her notebook.

    a. Possessive adjective: _____

    b. Possessor: _____

    c. Number of noun possessed: **El cuaderno** (*notebook*) is

    _____.

    Teresa perdió _____cuaderno.

2. Our teacher is from Colombia.

    a. Possessive adjective: _____

    b. Possessor: _____

    c. Gender and number of noun possessed: **La profesora** is

    _____

_____ profesora es de Colombia.

3. Andrew, where are your gloves?

    a. Possessive adjective: _____

    b. Possessor: _____

    c. Number of noun possessed: **Los guantes** (*gloves*) is

    _____

    Andrés, ¿dónde están _____ guantes?

4. They went to the movies with their father.

    a. Possessive adjective: _____

    b. Possessor: _____

    c. Number of noun possessed: **El padre** (*father*) is

    _____

    Fueron al cine con _____ padre.

5. Roberto went to the game with his father.

    a. Possessive adjective: _____

    b. Possessor: _____

    c. Number of noun possessed: **El padre** (*father*) is

    _____

    Roberto fue al partido con _____ padre.

What is an Interrogative Adjective?

An **interrogative adjective** is a word that asks a question about a noun.

In English: The words *which* and *what* are called interrogative adjectives when they come in front of a noun and are used to ask a question about that noun.

> *Which* instructor is teaching the course?
> *What* courses are you taking?

In Spanish: There are two interrogative adjectives: **qué** which corresponds to the English *which* or *what* and the forms **cuánto** meaning *how much* or *how many*.[1]

1. *Which* or *what* + noun = **qué** + noun

Qué is invariable; that is, it does not change form to agree in number and gender with the noun it modifies.

> ¿**Qué** revista lees?
> *What magazine are you reading?*

> ¿**Qué** libros quieres?
> *Which books do you want?*

2. *How much* or *how many* + noun = **cuánto** + noun

Cuánto has four forms to agree in gender and number with the noun it modifies.

---

[1] In certain areas of the Spanish-speaking word **cuál** and **cuáles** can function as interrogative adjectives: ¿**Cuál libro quieres?** However, **qué** is the interrogative adjective *which/what* used in standard Spanish.

How much money do you need?

> **El dinero** (*money*) is masculine singular
> so the word for "how much" must be
> masculine singular.

¿**Cuánto** dinero necesitas?
‌ ‌ ‌ ‌ └──┬──┘
‌ ‌ ‌ ‌ ‌ masc. sing.

How much soup do you want?

> **La sopa** (*soup*) is feminine singular
> so the word for "how much" must
> be feminine singular.

¿**Cuánta** sopa quieres?
‌ ‌ ‌ ‌ └──┬──┘
‌ ‌ ‌ ‌ ‌ fem. sing.

How many records do you have?

> **Los discos** (*records*) is masculine plural
> so the word for "how many" must be
> masculine plural.

¿**Cuántos** discos tienes?
‌ ‌ ‌ ‌ └──┬──┘
‌ ‌ ‌ ‌ ‌ masc. pl.

How many suitcases are you bringing?

> **Las maletas** (*suitcases*) is feminine
> plural so the word for "how many"
> must be feminine plural.

¿**Cuántas** maletas traes?
‌ ‌ ‌ ‌ └──┬──┘
‌ ‌ ‌ ‌ ‌ fem. pl.

NOTE: The word "what" is not always an interrogative adjective. In the question, "*What* is on the table?" *what* is an interrogative pronoun and as an interrogative pronoun **qué is** not followed by a noun: **¿Qué hay en la mesa?** The words "how many" in "*How many* do you need?" is also an interrogative pronoun; it is not followed by a noun: **¿Cuántos necesitas?** It is important to distinguish interrogative adjectives from interrogative pronouns because sometimes different words are used in Spanish. (See **What is an Interrogative Pronoun?**, p. 201.)

Practice

A. In the following sentences:
- Circle the interrogative adjectives.
- Draw an arrow from the interrogative adjective to the noun it modifies.

1. How much time do you need?

2. Which book is yours?

3. Please tell me what exercises are due tomorrow.

4. How many sisters do you have?

5. Which house do you live in?

B. In the following sentences:
- Circle the English interrogative adjectives.
- Fill in the blanks.

1. How many shirts did you buy?

    Las camisas (in English: _____) is feminine plural.

    ¿ _____ camisas compraste?

2. How much wine are you bringing to the party?

   El vino (in English: _____) is masculine singular.

   ¿ _____ vino traes a la fiesta?

3. How many telephones are there in your house?

   Los teléfonos (in English: _____) is masculine plural.

   ¿ _____ teléfonos hay en tu casa?

4. How much salad do you want?

   La ensalada (in English: _____) is feminine singular.

   ¿ _____ ensalada quieres?

What is a Demonstrative Adjective?

A **demonstrative adjective** is a word used to point out a person or an object.

In English: The demonstrative adjectives are *this* and *that* in the singular and *these* and *those* in the plural. They are rare examples of adjectives agreeing in number with the noun they modify; *this* changes to *these* and *that* changes to *those* when they modify a plural noun.

SINGULAR	PLURAL
this cat	*these* cats
that man	*those* men

This and *these* refer to a person or object near the speaker, and *that* and *those* refer to a person or object away from the speaker.

In Spanish: There are three sets of demonstrative adjectives that change to agree in gender and number with the nouns they modify. In order to say "this house" or "that room" you start by determining where the person or object is in relation to the speaker or the person spoken to. Then, determine the gender and number of the noun you wish to point out and make the demonstrative adjective agree with that noun.

1. To point out nouns near the speaker (*this, these*), use a form of este

> *this room*   **este** cuarto
>   masc. sing.
>
> *this house*   **esta** casa
>   fem. sing.
>
> *these rooms*   **estos** cuartos
>   masc. pl.
>
> *these houses*   **estas** casas
>   fem. pl.

To say "this book" in Spanish analyze the Spanish equivalent for the word "book."

> *Do you see **this** book?*
>
> > **El libro** (*book*) is masculine singular so the word for *this* must also be masculine singular.
>
> ¿Ves **este** libro?
>   masc. sing.

Similarly, to say "these tables" begin by analyzing the Spanish equivalent for the word "tables."

*Do you see **these** tables?*

> **Las mesas** (*tables*) is feminine plural so the word
> for *these* must also be feminine plural.

¿Ves **estas** mesas?
|___|___|
   fem. pl.

2. To point out nouns near the person spoken to (*that, those*), use a form of **ese**

that room	**ese** cuarto
	masc. sing.
that house	**esa** casa
	fem. sing.
those rooms	**esos** cuartos
	masc. pl.
those houses	**esas** casas
	fem. pl.

If you want to say "that table" in Spanish, begin by analyzing the Spanish equivalent for *table*.

*Do you see **that** table?*

> **La mesa** (*table*) is feminine singular, so the
> word for *that* must also be feminine singular.

¿Ves **esa** mesa?
|___|___|
   fem. sing.

Similarly, if you want to say "those books" begin by analyzing the Spanish equivalent for *books*.

>   *Do you see **those** books?*
>
>   Los libros (*books*) is masculine plural, so the
>   word for *those* must also be masculine plural.
>
>   ¿Ves **esos** libros?
>   └─┬─┘
>   masc. pl.

3. To point out nouns away from both the speaker and the person spoken to (*that, those*), use a form of **aquel**

>   *that room*   **aquel** cuarto
>   └──┬──┘
>   masc. sing.
>
>   *that house*   **aquella** casa
>   └──┬──┘
>   fem. sing.
>
>   *those rooms*   **aquellos** cuartos
>   └──┬──┘
>   masc. pl.
>
>   *those houses*   **aquellas** casas
>   └──┬──┘
>   fem. pl.

Since English does not have this third set of demonstrative adjectives, there is no good translation for them. Sometimes the forms of **aquel** translate as "that/those over there" to imply distance: **aquella casa** = *that house over there.*

If you want to say "those tables over there" in Spanish, begin by analyzing the Spanish equivalent for *tables*.

Do you see those tables over there?

> **Las mesas** (*tables*) is feminine plural so the
> word for *those* must also be feminine plural.

¿Ves **aquellas** mesas?

fem. pl.

NOTE: The three sets of demonstrative adjectives may also function as demonstrative pronouns. As demonstrative pronouns they
are not followed by a noun and they carry a written accent. (See
What is a Demonstrative Pronoun?, p. 212.)

Practice

A. In the following sentences:
  • Circle the demonstrative adjective.
  • Draw an arrow from the demonstrative adjective to the noun it
    modifies.

1. They prefer that restaurant.

2. I bought these jeans on sale.

3. Those houses are very expensive.

4. Do you want this magazine?

B. In the following sentences:
  • Circle the demonstrative adjective.
  • Fill in the blanks.

1. Where did you buy that dress you're wearing?

   a. Relationship of noun modified to speaker or person spoken

      to: _____

b. Demonstrative adjective needed: _____

c. Gender of noun modified: masculine

d. Number of noun modified: _____

¿Dónde compraste _____ vestido que llevas?

2. This table is very expensive.

a. Relationship of noun modified to speaker or person spoken

to: _____

b. Demonstrative adjective needed: _____

c. Gender of noun modified: feminine

d. Number of noun modified: _____

_____ mesa es muy cara.

3. Those mountains over there are beautiful.

a. Relationship of noun modified to speaker or person spoken

to: _____

b. Demonstrative adjective needed: _____

c. Gender of noun modified: feminine

d. Number of noun modified: _____

_____ montañas son hermosas.

What is Meant by Comparison of Adjectives?

We compare adjectives when two or more nouns have the same quality, and we want to indicate that one of these nouns has a greater, lesser, or equal degree of this quality.

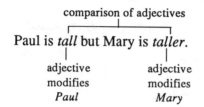

There are two types of comparison: comparative and superlative.

In English: Let us go over what is meant by the different types of comparison and how each type is formed.

1. The **comparative** compares a quality of one person or thing with the same quality in another person or thing. The comparison can indicate that one or the other has more, less, or the same amount of the quality.

   The comparison of greater degree (more) is formed:

   • short adjective + *-er* + *than*

      Paul is tall*er than* Mary.
      Susan is old*er than* her sister.

   • *more* + longer adjective + *than*

      Mary is *more* intelligent *than* John.
      My car is *more* expensive *than* your car.

The comparison of lesser degree (less) is formed:

- *less* + adjective + *than*

  John is *less* intelligent *than* Mary.
  Your car is *less* expensive *than* my car.

The comparison of equal degree (same) is formed:

- *(not) as* + adjective + *as*

  Robert is *as* intelligent *as* Mary.
  My car is *not as* expensive *as* his car.

2. The **superlative** is used to stress the highest and lowest degrees of a quality.

   The superlative of highest degree is formed:

   - *the* + short adjective + *-est*

     Anita is *the* short*est*.
     Their house is *the* cheap*est* on the block.

   - *the most* + long adjective

     Mary is *the most* intelligent.
     Her car is *the most* expensive of all.

   The superlative of lowest degree degree is formed:

   - *the least* + adjective

     Anita is *the least* tall.
     Your car is *the least* expensive of all.

A few adjectives do not follow this regular pattern of comparison. You must use an entirely different form for the comparative and the superlative.

ADJECTIVE	This apple is *good*.
COMPARATIVE	This apple is *better*.
	not "gooder"
SUPERLATIVE	This apple is *the best*.
	not "goodest"

In Spanish: There are the same two types of comparison of adjectives as in English: comparative and superlative. Remember that agreement between the adjective and noun is always required.

1. The comparative of two unequal qualities is formed with the phrase **más** (*more*) or **menos** (*less*) + adjective + **que** (*than*).

   María es **más** alta **que** Roberto.
   *Mary is **taller than** Robert.*

   Mi coche es **menos** caro **que** el tuyo.
   *My car is **less** expensive **than** yours.*

   The comparative of equal qualities is formed with the phrase **tan** (*as*) + adjective + **como** (*as*).

   María es **tan** alta **como** Juan.
   *Mary is **as tall as** John.*

2. The superlative is formed by **el, la, los, las** (depending on the gender and number of the noun described) + **más** (*most*) or **menos** (*least*) + adjective.

Juan es **el más** bajo de la familia.
masc. sing.

*John is **the shortest** in the family.*

María es **la más** alta.
fem. sing.

*Mary is **the tallest**.*

Carlos y Roberto son **los más** divertidos de la clase.
masc. pl.

*Charles and Robert are **the funniest** in the class.*

Teresa y Gloria son **las más** inteligentes.
fem. pl.

*Teresa and Gloria are **the most** intelligent.*

Mi coche es **el menos** caro.
masc. sing.

*My car is **the least** expensive.*

As in English, a few adjectives have irregular forms of comparison which you will have to memorize individually.

ADJECTIVE	Esta manzana es **buena**. *This apple is **good**.*
COMPARATIVE	Esta manzana es **mejor**. *This apple is **better**.*

SUPERLATIVE   Esta manzana es **la mejor.**
                                     This apple is the best.

NOTE: Adverbs (see **What is an Adverb?**, p. 162) are compared in the same manner as adjectives in both English and Spanish.

Practice

A. Using the elements given, write sentences with comparative adjectives. The various degrees of comparison are indicated as follows:

        + + superlative   = equal degree
        + greater degree   − lesser degree

1. The teacher is / (+) old / the students

_____

2. He is / (−) intelligent / I am

_____

3. Mary is / (=) tall / Paul

_____

4. That boy is / (+ +) bad / in the school

_____

5. Paul is a / (+) good student / Tom

_____

B. If you had to write the following sentences in Spanish, you would have to determine whether to use **el, la, los** or **las** to form the superlative.

   • Circle the noun you would have to analyze.

1. Paul wrote the best composition.

2. She did the least difficult exercises.

3. Mary is certainly the friendliest girl in the class.

4. Paul is the most diligent and least talkative student.

What is an Adverb?

An **adverb** is a word that describes a verb, an adjective, or another adverb. Adverbs indicate quantity, time, place, intensity, and manner.

Mary drives *well.*
|
verb

The house is *very* big.
|
adjective

The girl ran *too* quickly.
|
adverb

In English: Here are some examples of types of adverbs:

- of manner

    These adverbs answer the question *how?* They are the most common adverbs and can usually be recognized by their *-ly* ending.

    Mary sings *beautifully.*
    They parked the car *carefully.*

- of quantity or degree

    These adverbs answer the question *how much?*

    > Mary sleeps *little* these days.
    > Paul does *well* enough in class.

- of time

    These adverbs answer the question *when?*

    > He will be home *soon.*
    > The children arrived *late.*

- of place

    These adverbs answer the question *where?*

    > The teacher looked *around.*
    > The old were left *behind.*

- of intensity

    These adverbs are used for *emphasis.*

    > These are *really* beautiful.
    > Mary can *actually* read Latin.

In Spanish: You will have to memorize most adverbs as vocabulary items. Most adverbs of manner can be recognized by their ending **-mente** which corresponds to the English ending *-ly*.

natural**mente**	*naturally*
general**mente**	*generally*
rápida**mente**	*rapidly*

The most important fact for you to remember is that adverbs are **invariable**; this means they never change their form. (Adverbs never become plural, nor do they have gender.)

Because adverbs are invariable and adjectives must agree with the noun they modify, you must be able to distinguish one from the other. When you write a sentence in Spanish, always make sure that adjectives agree with the nouns or pronouns they modify and that adverbs remain unchanged.

> The **tall** girl talked **rapidly**.

>> *Tall* modifies the noun *girl;* it is an adjective.
>> *Rapidly* modifies the verb *talked;* it describes
>> how she talked; it is an adverb.

> La chica **alta** habló **rápidamente.**
> fem. sing.   adverb

> The **tall** boy talked **rapidly**.

>> *Tall* modifies the noun *boy;* it is an adjective.
>> *Rapidly* modifies the verb *talked;* it
>> describes how he talked; it is an adverb.

> El chico **alto** habló **rápidamente.**
> masc. sing.   adverb

Remember that in English *good* is an adjective; *well* is an adverb.

> The boy is *good.* (He behaves properly.)

>> *Good* modifies the noun *boy;* it is therefore an adjective.

> The boy is *well.* (He isn't sick.)

>> *Well* modifies the verb *is;* it is therefore an adverb.

Likewise, in Spanish **bueno** is an adjective meaning *good;* **bien** is
the adverb meaning *well.*

*The **good** students speak Spanish w**e**ll.*
 adjective   adverb

Los estudiantes **buenos** hablan español **bien.**
 masc. pl.   adverb

Adverbs are compared in the same manner as adjectives (see **What is
Meant by Comparison of Adjectives?**, p. 157).

Practice

In the following sentences:
- Circle the adverbs.
- Draw an arrow from the adverb to the word it modifies.

1. The students arrived early.

2. Paul learned the lesson really quickly.

3. The students were too tired to study.

4. He has a reasonably secure income.

5. Mary is a good student who speaks Spanish very well.

What is a Conjunction?

A **conjunction** is a word that links words or groups of words.

In English: There are two kinds of conjunctions: coordinating and subordinating.

1. **Coordinating conjunctions** join words, phrases, and clauses that are equal; they *coordinate* elements of equal rank. The major coordinating conjunctions are *and, but, or, nor, for,* and *yet.*

   > good *or* evil
   > over the river *and* through the woods
   > They invited us, *but* we couldn't go.

2. **Subordinating conjunctions** join a dependent clause to a main clause; they subordinate one clause to another. A clause introduced by a subordinating conjunction is called a **subordinate clause**. Typical subordinating conjunctions are *before, after, since, although, because, if, unless, so that, while, that,* and *when.*

   > *Although* we were invited, we didn't go.
   > | |_____|
   > subordinating   main clause
   > conjunction

   > They left *because* they were bored.
   > |___| |
   > main clause   subordinating
   >   conjunction

   > He said *that* he was tired.
   > |___| |
   > main clause   subordinating
   >   conjunction

Notice that the subordinate clause may come either at the beginning of the sentence or after the main clause.

In Spanish: Conjunctions must be memorized as vocabulary items. Remember that, like adverbs and prepositions, conjunctions are invariable; that is, they never change their form.

Practice

In the following sentences:
- Circle the coordinating and subordinating conjunctions.
- Underline the words each conjunction serves to coordinate or to subordinate.

1. Mary and Paul were going to study French or Spanish.

2. She did not study because she was too tired.

3. Not only had he forgotten his ticket, but he had forgotten his passport as well.

4. She knew he was mean, yet she still loved him.

5. They borrowed money so they could go to Mexico.

What is a Preposition?

A **preposition** is a word that shows the relationship of one word (usually a noun or pronoun) to another word in the sentence. The noun or pronoun following the preposition is called the **object of the preposition**. The preposition plus its object is called a **prepositional phrase**. Prepositions normally indicate position, direction, or time.

In English: Here are examples of some prepositions showing:

- position

> Paul was *in* the car.
> Mary put the books *on* the table.

- direction

> Mary went *to* school.
> The students came directly *from* class.

- time

> Spanish people go on vacation *in* August.
> *Before* class, they went to eat.

Not all prepositions are single words:

because of	in front of	instead of
due to	in spite of	on account of

In Spanish: You will have to memorize prepositions as vocabulary items. Their meaning and use must be carefully studied. There are three important things to remember:

1. Prepositions are invariable. This means they never change their form. (They never become plural, nor do they have a gender.)

2. Prepositions are tricky little words. Every language uses prepositions differently. Do not assume that the same preposition is used in Spanish as in English, or even that a preposition will be used in Spanish when you must use one in English (and vice versa).

ENGLISH	SPANISH
CHANGE OF PREPOSITIONS	
to laugh *at*	reirse **de** (*of*)
to consist *of*	consistir **en** (*in*)

PREPOSITION	NO PREPOSITION
to look *for*	buscar
to look *at*	mirar

NO PREPOSITION	PREPOSITION
to leave	salir **de**
to enter	entrar **en**

A good dictionary will usually give you the verb plus the preposition when one is required. In particular, be careful not to translate an English verb + preposition word-for-word. For example, when you consult the dictionary to find the Spanish equivalent of *look for*, do not stop at the first entry for *look* (which is **mirar**) and then add the preposition **para** (corresponding to *for*). Continue searching for the specific meaning *look for* (which corresponds to the verb **buscar** used without a preposition).

> *I am looking for my keys.*
> **Busco** mis llaves.

On the other hand, when looking up a verb such as **entrar** (*to enter*), be sure to include the Spanish preposition **en** which you should find listed in the entry.

> *Mary **enters** the living room.*
> María **entra en** la sala.

3. Although the position of a preposition in an English sentence may vary, it cannot in Spanish. Spoken English often places a preposition at the end of the sentence; in this position it is called a **dangling preposition**. In formal English there is a strong tendency to avoid dangling prepositions by placing them within the sentence or at the beginning of a question.

SPOKEN ENGLISH ───────────▶ FORMAL ENGLISH

The man I spoke to is Spanish.	The man to whom I spoke is Spanish.
Who are you playing with?	With whom are you playing?
Here is the girl you asked about.	Here is the girl about whom you asked.

Spanish places prepositions the same way as formal English; that is, within the sentence or at the beginning of a question. A preposition is never placed at the end of a Spanish sentence.

> Roberto es el hombre **a quien le** hablé ayer.
> *Roberto is the man to whom I spoke yesterday.*

> ¿**Con quién** juegas?
> *With whom are you playing?*

There are some English expressions where the natural position of the preposition is at the end of the sentence; it is not a question of the difference in spoken or formal language.

> What are you thinking *about*?

Changing the structure by placing the preposition within the sentence would sound awkward.

> *About what* are you thinking?

However, as awkward as it may sound in English, this is the structure that must be used in the Spanish sentence.

> ¿**En qué** piensas?

PREPOSITION *DE*

A special word needs to be said about the Spanish preposition **de** (*of, from*) because it is used in so many common Spanish expressions.

1. When a noun is used as an adjective to describe another noun (see p. 136), **de** is used as follows:

   • the noun described + **de** + the describing noun used without an article

	A	B		B	A
	los libros **de** química			*the chemistry books*	
	la clase **de** español			*the Spanish class*	
	el aceite **de** oliva			*the olive oil*	

   The noun in Column B describes the noun in Column A. Notice how the describing noun comes after **de** and the described noun in Spanish, while it comes before the described noun in English.

2. When indicating the quantity of a noun, **de** is used as follows:

   • the quantity + **de** + the noun without an article

   una docena **de** huevos   *a dozen eggs*
   un par **de** guantes   *a pair of gloves*
   un kilo **de** jamón   *a kilo of ham*

3. When a noun possesses another noun (see p. 19) **de** is used as follows:

   • the noun possessed + **de** + definite or indefinite article + the noun that possesses

   A   B   B   A
   el coche **del** señor   *the man's car*
                 |
            de + el

   el vestido **de la** mujer   *the woman's dress*
   los discos **de los** chicos   *the boys' records*
   la casa **de las** hermanas   *the sisters' house*
   las ramas **de un** árbol   *the branches of a tree*

The noun in Column A belongs to the noun in Column B. Notice how the possessed noun comes before the possessor in Spanish, while it comes after in English. The Spanish structure parallels the English structure *the car of the man, the dress of the woman, the records of the boys, the house of the sisters,* and *the branches of a tree.*

Practice

A. Circle the prepositions in the following sentences.

1. The students didn't understand what the lesson was about.

2. The professor had come from Peru by boat.

3. The teacher walked around the room as she talked.

4. Contrary to popular opinion he was a good student.

5. The garden between the two houses was very small.

B. The following are sentences in informal English.
   • On the line below each sentence, write the restructured sentence that parallels the structure of the Spanish sentence.

1. Whose car are you riding in?

_____

2. I got the scholarship I applied for.

_____

3. Which movie is John going to?

_____

4. Richard is the boy I was talking about.

_____

What are Objects?

Every sentence consists, at the very least, of a subject and a verb. This is called the **sentence base**.

> Children play.
> Work stoppped.

The subject of the sentence is usually a noun or pronoun. Many sentences contain other nouns or pronouns that are related to the action of the verb or to a preposition. These nouns or pronouns are called **objects**.

> Paul writes a letter.
> subject | object
> verb

> He speaks to Mary.
> subject | object
> verb

> Paul goes out with Mary.
> subject | object
> verb

There are three types of objects:

1. direct object
2. indirect object
3. object of a preposition

1. AND 2. DIRECT AND INDIRECT OBJECTS

In English: Let us see how these two types of objects are identified in English.

1. **Direct object:** It is a noun or pronoun that receives the action of the verb directly, without a preposition. It answers the question *what?* or *whom?* asked after the verb.[1]

> Paul writes *a letter.*
>
>> Paul writes what? A letter.
>> *A letter* is the direct object.
>
> They see *Paul and Mary.*
>
>> They see whom? Paul and Mary.
>> *Paul and Mary* are the two direct objects.

Do not assume thay any word that comes right after a verb is automatically the direct object. It must answer the question *what?* or *whom?*

> Paul sees well.
>
>> Paul see *what?* No answer.
>> Paul sees *whom?* No answer.

There is no direct object in the sentence. *Well* is an adverb; it answers the question: Paul sees *how?*

2. **Indirect object:** It is a noun or pronoun that receives the action of the verb indirectly. It answers the two-word question *to whom?* or *to what?* asked after the verb.

> John writes *his brother.*
>
>> John writes to whom? To his brother.
>> *His brother* is the indirect object.

---

[1] In this section, we will consider active sentences only. (See **What is Meant by Active and Passive Voice?**, p. 125.)

Sometimes the word *to* is included in the English sentence.[1]

> John speaks *to Paul and Mary*.
>
>> John speaks to whom? To Paul and Mary.
>> *Paul and Mary* are the two indirect objects.

A sentence may contain both a direct object and an indirect object. In English, when both objects are present, the indirect object usually precedes the direct object, but without the preposition *to*.

> Paul gave *his sister* a gift.
>
>> *His sister* answers the question *to whom?* and is
>> the indirect object in the sentence, even though
>> the preposition "to" does not appear.

When a sentence has both a direct and indirect object, the following two word orders are possible:

- subject (s) + verb (v) + indirect object (io) + direct object (do)

> Paul gave his sister a gift.
> S   V   IO   DO
>
>> Who gave a gift? Paul.
>> *Paul* is the subject.
>
>> Paul gave *what*? A gift.
>> *A gift* is the direct object.
>
>> Paul gave a gift *to whom?* His sister.
>> *His sister* is the indirect object.

---

[1] In English "to Paul and Mary" is called a prepositional phrase because it is a phrase that begins with the preposition *to;* in this book we refer to phrases like "to Paul and Mary" as indirect objects since that is how they function in Spanish.

- subject + verb + direct object + *to* + indirect object

Paul gave a gift to his sister.
  | | | |
 S   V   DO   IO

Note that although the word order changes, the function of each word does not. Be sure that you ask the questions to establish the functions of the words in a sentence.

In Spanish: Direct and indirect objects are related to the verb in the same way they are in English.

1. Direct object: it answers the one-word question *what?* or *whom?* asked after the verb.

> Pablo escribe **una carta.**
> *Paul writes **a letter.***

In Spanish when the direct object of the verb is a person, it is preceded by the word **a**. This is called the **personal a**.

> Juan ve **a las muchachas.**
> |
>
> personal **a** followed by a direct object
> noun referring to persons

*John sees **the girls.***

> Juan ve **al hombre.**
> |

> personal **a** followed by a direct object noun
> referring to persons

*John sees **the man.***

Juan ve **la casa.**

> direct object noun referring to a thing;
> no personal **a** included.

*John sees **the house**.*

2. Indirect object: It answers the two-word question *to whom?* or *to what?* asked after the verb. The English word *to* is expressed by **a** in Spanish. The indirect object pronouns **le** or **les** must always be used even though the indirect object noun is also included in the sentence. **Le** is used when the indirect object noun is singular and **les** is used when the indirect object noun is plural.

Juan **le** escribe **a su hermano.**

> singular

*John writes **(to) his brother**.*

Juan **les** habla **a Pablo y a María.**

> plural

*John speaks **to Paul and Mary**.*

Direct or Indirect Object

It is essential that you learn to distinguish direct and indirect objects especially when dealing with pronouns. Since the "**a**" is used not only before an indirect object but also before a direct object referring to a person, it is often difficult to distinguish the two types of objects in a Spanish sentence.

It is often possible to use the English sentence as a guide. Ask yourself if the English sentence contains or could contain the word *to* before the object. If yes, it is an indirect object; if not, it is a direct object.

Juan le habla **a María.**

> Can the word *to* be placed before the object? Yes.
> John speaks *to* Mary.
> *Mary* is the indirect object.

Juan les escribe **a sus amigos.**

> Can the word *to* be placed before the object? Yes.
> John writes *to* his friends.
> *His friends* is the indirect object.

Juan ve a María.

> Can the word *to* be placed before the object? No.
> John sees Mary.
> "John sees to Mary" cannot exist in English.
> *Mary* is the direct object.

When a Spanish sentence contains both a direct and an indirect object, there is only one word order possible: the direct object noun precedes the indirect object noun. (Pronoun objects follow a different word order.)

• subject + **le / les** + verb + direct object + **a** + indirect object

> Pablo **le** escribe **una carta a su hermano.**
> *Paul writes a letter to his brother.*

When expressing a sentence with double objects in Spanish, remember to restructure the English sentence so the direct object noun precedes the indirect object noun. Then translate the sentence into Spanish.

> *Martha gave **the girl a present.***
> | |
> indirect obj.   direct obj.

> *Martha gave **a present to the girl.***
> | |
> direct obj.   indirect obj.

Marta le dio un regalo a la muchacha.
        | |
   direct obj.   indirect object

3. OBJECT OF A PREPOSITION

In English: An **object of a preposition** is a noun or pronoun that follows a preposition and is related to it. It answers the question *what?* or *whom?* asked after the preposition.

> Paul is leaving *with Mary.*
>
> > With whom? With Mary.
> > *Mary* is the object of the preposition *with.*
>
> He works *for Mr. Jones.*
>
> > For whom? For Mr. Jones.
> > *Mr. Jones* is the object of the preposition *for.*

In Spanish: Objects of a preposition are as easy to identify as in English.

> Pablo sale **con María.**
> *Paul is leaving **with Mary.***
>
> Trabaja **para el Sr. Jones.**
> *He works for Mr. Jones.*

OBJECTS IN ENGLISH AND SPANISH

The relationship between verb and object are often different in English and Spanish. For example, a verb may take an object of a preposition in English but a direct object in Spanish. For this reason, it is important that you pay close attention to such differences when you learn Spanish verbs. Your textbook, as well as dictionaries, will indicate when a Spanish verb is followed by a preposition.

Here are some examples of the kinds of differences that you are most likely to encounter.

Object of a preposition in English ⟶ Direct object in Spanish

I am looking for the book.

> Function in English: object of a preposition
> I am looking for what? The book.
> *The book* is the object of the preposition *for*.

Busco **el libro.**

> Function in Spanish: direct object
> **¿Qué busco? El libro.**
> Since **buscar** is not followed by a preposition,
> it takes a direct object.

Here is a list of a few common verbs that require an object of a preposition in English but a direct object in Spanish.

to look for	buscar
to look at	mirar
to ask for	pedir
to listen to	escuchar
to wait for	esperar
to wait on	servir

Direct object in English ⟶ Object of a preposition in Spanish

*John remembers **his apartment** in Madrid.*

> Function in English: direct object
> John remembers what? His apartment.
> *His apartment* is the direct object.

Juan se acuerda **de su apartamento** en Madrid.

> Function in Spanish: object of a preposition
> **¿De qué se acuerda Juan? De su apartamento.**
> The verb is **acordarse de** and it requires an object
> for the preposition **de**.

Here is a list of a few common verbs that require a direct object in English but an object of a preposition in Spanish.

to enjoy	gozar **de**
to enter	entrar **en**
to forget	olvidarse **de**
to leave	salir **de**
to marry	casarse **con**
to play	jugar **a**
to remember	acordarse **de**

Always identify the function of a word within the language in which you are working; do not mix English patterns into Spanish.

SUMMARY

The different types of objects in a sentence can be identified by looking to see if they are introduced by a preposition and, if so, by which one.

An object that receives the action of the verb directly, without a preposition, is called direct.

An object that receives the action of the verb indirectly, sometimes with the preposition *to*, is called indirect.

An object that is related to a preposition is called the object of a preposition.

Your ability to recognize the three kinds of objects is essential when using pronouns. As you will see in the following section, different pronouns are used for the English pronoun *him* depending on whether *him* is a direct object (**lo**), an indirect object (**le**), or an object of a preposition (**él**).

Practice

Find the objects in the following sentences.
- Next to Q, write the question you need to ask to find the object.
- Next to A, write the answer to the question you just asked.
- In the column to the right, identify the kind of object it is by circling the appropriate letters: Direct object (DO), Indirect object (IO), or Object of a preposition (OP)

1. The children took a shower.

   Q: _____

   A: _____   DO   IO   OP

2. They ate the meal with pleasure.

   Q: _____

   A: _____   DO   IO   OP

3. He sent his brother a present.

   Q: _____

   A: _____   DO   IO   OP

   Q: _____

   A: _____   DO   IO   OP

4. The parents paid for the books with a credit card.

   Q: _____

   A: _____   DO   IO   OP

   Q: _____

   A: _____   DO   IO   OP

What is an Object Pronoun?

An **object pronoun** is a pronoun used as an object of a verb or a preposition.

In English: Pronouns change according to their function in the sentence. Pronouns used as subjects are studied in **What is a Subject Pronoun?**, p. 37. We use subject pronouns when we learn to conjugate verbs (see **What is a Verb Conjugation?**, p. 49). In this section we shall look at pronouns used as objects. Object pronouns are used when a pronoun is either a direct object, indirect object, or object of a preposition. (See **What are Objects?**, p. 173.)

> She saw *me*.
> |
> direct object = object pronoun

> I lent *him* my car.
> |
> indirect object = object pronoun

> They went out with *her*.
> |
> object of a preposition = object pronoun

Compare the subject and object pronouns:

		SUBJECT	OBJECT
SINGULAR			
	1st PERSON	I	me
	2nd PERSON	you	you
		he	him
	3rd PERSON	she	her
		it	it
PLURAL			
	1st PERSON	we	us
	2nd PERSON	you	you
	3rd PERSON	they	them

The form of the object pronoun is the same whether the pronoun is used as a direct object, indirect object, or object of a preposition.

In Spanish: Different object pronouns are used for each kind of object: direct, indirect, and object of a preposition. You will, therefore, have to learn how to analyze them and how to choose the correct Spanish form.

A. DIRECT AND INDIRECT OBJECT PRONOUNS

Let us look at each of the English pronouns and see how to find the Spanish equivalent.

1. 1st and 2nd person singular and plural (*me, you, us*)

The Spanish equivalents have the same forms when they are used as direct and indirect object pronouns.

	SUBJECT	DIRECT AND INDIRECT OBJECT
SINGULAR 1st PERSON	yo	me
2nd PERSON	tú	te
PLURAL 1st PERSON	nosotros(-as)	nos
2nd PERSON	vosotros(-as)	os

Once you have established that a 1st or 2nd person pronoun is either a direct or indirect object, you merely have to place the correct form of the pronoun in front of the conjugated Spanish verb.

*John sees **me**.*

> John sees whom? Me.
> *Me* is the direct object pronoun.

Juan **me** ve.
$\quad\quad$|
$\quad\quad$direct object pronoun

*John speaks **to me**.*

> John speaks to whom? To me.
> *Me* is the indirect object pronoun.

Juan **me** habla.
$\quad\quad$|
$\quad\quad$indirect object pronoun

NOTE: The "to" preceding the English indirect object is not expressed in Spanish when a pronoun is used. The Spanish indirect object pronoun means *to me, to you*, etc.; there is no need for the equivalent of *to*.

2. 3rd person singular and plural (*him, her, you, it, them*)

The Spanish equivalents have a different form depending on whether they are used as direct or indirect objects. The direct object pronoun has four forms; a different form is used depending on the gender and number of the pronoun. The indirect object

	SUBJECT	DIRECT OBJECT	INDIRECT OBJECT
SINGULAR			
MASCULINE	él	lo	le
FEMININE	ella	la	le
YOU	usted	lo, la	le
PLURAL			
MASCULINE	ellos	los	les
FEMININE	ellas	las	les
YOU	ustedes	los, las	les

pronoun has two forms depending whether the pronoun is singular or plural.

An analysis of the following sentences, in which we have used each of the 3rd person English object pronouns, will enable us to select the proper Spanish form from the chart above.

Him—Always masculine singular; refers to a person. You will have to determine whether this pronoun is a direct or indirect object.

> *Do you see Paul? Yes, I see **him.***
>> 1. Function: direct object
>>   You see whom? Him.
>> 2. Selection: **lo**
>
> ¿Ves a Pablo? Sí, **lo** veo.

> *Are you giving Paul the book? Yes, I'm giving **him** the book.*
>> 1. Function: indirect object
>>   You are giving the book to whom? To him.
>> 2. Selection: **le**
>
> ¿Le das el libro a Pablo? Sí, **le** doy el libro.

Her—Always feminine singular; refers to a person. You have to determine whether this pronoun is a direct or indirect object.

> *Do you see Mary? Yes, I see **her.***
>> 1. Function: direct object
>>   You see whom? Her.
>> 2. Selection: **la**
>
> ¿Ves a María? Sí, **la** veo.

*Are you giving Mary the book? Yes, I am giving **her** the
book.*

    1. Function: indirect object
       You are giving the book to whom? To Mary.
    2. Selection: **le**

¿Le das el libro a María? Sí, **le** doy el libro.

You—Formal singular. You will have to determine whether this
pronoun is a direct or indirect object. If it is a direct object, you
will also need to determine whether the antecedent is masculine
or feminine.

*Whom does Paul see? He sees **you.***
                                     masculine

    1. Function: direct object
       Paul sees whom? You.
    2. Selection: **lo**

¿A quién ve Pablo? Pablo **lo** ve.

*Whom does Paul see? He sees **you.***
                                    feminine

    1. Function: direct object
       Paul sees whom? You.
    2. Selection: **la**

¿A quién ve Pablo? Pablo **la** ve.

*To whom does Paul give the book? Paul gives **you** the
book.*

    1. Function: indirect object
       Paul gives the book to whom? To you.
    2. Selection: **le**

¿A quién le da el libro Pablo? Pablo **le** da el libro a Ud.

In order to distinguish **le** meaning *to him* from **le** meaning *to her* or *to you*, the phrase **a él, a ella** or **a usted** can be added to the end of the sentence.

Le doy el libro **a él.**	*I am giving the book to him.*
Le doy el libro **a ella.**	*I am giving the book to her.*
Le doy el libro **a usted.**	*I am giving the book to you.*

It—Always singular, always refers to a thing. You will have to determine whether this pronoun is a direct or indirect object. If is a direct object, you will have to determine whether its antecedent is masculine or feminine.

Do you see the book? Yes, I see it.

    1. Function: direct object
       You see what? It.
    2. Antecedent: **El libro** (*book*) is masculine.
    3. Selection: **lo**

¿Ves el libro? Sí, **lo** veo.

Do you see the table? Yes, I see it.

    1. Function: direct object
       You see what? It.
    2. Antecedent: **La mesa** (*table*) is feminine.
    3. Selection: **la**

¿Ves la mesa? Sí, **la** veo.

Are you giving money to the club? Yes, I am giving money to it.

    1. Function: indirect object
       You are giving to what? To the club.
    2. Selection: **le**

¿Le das dinero al club? Sí, **le** doy dinero.

Them—Always plural; refers to persons and things. You will have to determine whether this pronoun is a direct or indirect object. If it is a direct object, you will also need to determine whether the antecedent is masculine or feminine.

> *Do you see the girls? Yes, I see them.*
>> 1. Function: direct object
>>   You see whom? The girls.
>> 2. Antecedent: **Las chicas** (*girls*) is feminine.
>> 3. Selection: **las**

¿Ves a las chicas? Sí, **las** veo.

> *Do you see the cars? Yes, I see them.*
>> 1. Function: direct object
>>   You see what? The cars.
>> 2. Antecedent: **Los coches** (*cars*) is masculine.
>> 3. Selection: **los**

¿Ves los coches? Sí, **los** veo.

> *Do you give money to those groups? Yes, I give them money.*
>> 1. Function: indirect object
>>   You give to what? To them.
>> 2. Selection: **les**

¿Les das dinero a esos grupos? Sí, **les** doy dinero.

In order to distinguish **les** meaning *to them* (masculine or feminine) and *to you,* the phrase **a ellos, a ellas,** or **a ustedes** can be added to the end of the sentence.

> *John gave **them** the money.*
> |
>   feminine

Juan **les** dio el dinero **a ellas.**

*John gave **you** the money.*
Juan **les** dio el dinero **a ustedes.**

B. PRONOUNS AS OBJECTS OF PREPOSITIONS

Pronouns that are objects of prepositions other than *to* have forms that are different from the forms used as direct or indirect objects. Unlike other object pronouns which are placed before the verb, pronouns used as objects of prepositions are placed after the preposition. In this they are like nouns used as objects of prepositions.

Let us look at each of the English pronouns and see how to find the Spanish equivalent.

	SUBJECT	OBJECT OF PREPOSITION
SINGULAR		
1st PERSON	yo	mí
2nd PERSON	tú	ti
3rd PERSON	él / ella / usted	él / ella / usted
PLURAL		
1st PERSON	nosotros(-as)	nosotros(-as)
2nd PERSON	vosotros(-as)	vosotros(-as)
3rd PERSON	ellos / ellas / ustedes	ellos / ellas / ustedes

NOTE: The subject and object of preposition pronouns are alike except for the 1st and 2nd person singular.

1. 1st and 2nd persons singular and plural *(me, you, us, you)*

Once you have established that a 1st or 2nd person singular pronoun is an object of a preposition, you merely have to write down the preposition followed by the correct pronoun object. In the plural forms you will need to determine the gender of the pronoun as well.

> *Is the book for John? No, it's for me.*
> *No, it's for you.*
> |
>   fam. sing.

    1. Function: object of preposition *for*
    2. Selection: **mí**
               ti

> ¿Es el libro para Juan? No, es para **mí**.
> No, es para **ti**.

> *Is the book for John? No, it's for us.*
> |
>   masc.

> *No, it's for us.*
> |
>   fem.

> *No, it's for you.*
> |
>   masc. pl.

> *No, it's for you.*
> |
>   fem. pl.

    1. Function: object of preposition *for*
    2. Selection: **nosotros**
               nosotras
               vosotros
               vosotras

> ¿Es el libro para Juan? No, es para **nosotros**.
> No, es para **nosotras**.
> No, es para **vosotros**.
> No, es para **vosotras**.

2. 3rd person singular and plural (*him, her, it, them, you*)

The Spanish equivalents have a different form depending on the gender and number of the pronoun.

An analysis of the following sentences in which we have used each of the 3rd person object of preposition pronouns will enable us to select the proper Spanish form.

Him and *Her*—*Him* is always masculine singular and *her* is always feminine singular. You only have to establish whether these pronouns are objects of a preposition.

> *Is the book for Paul? Yes, it is for* **him.**
> *Is the book for Mary? Yes, it is for* **her.**
>
> > 1. Function: object of preposition *for*
> > 2. Selection: **él**
> >   **ella**

> ¿Es el libro para Juan? Sí, es para **él.**
> ¿Es el libro para María? Sí, es para **ella.**

It—In Spanish a noun referring to a thing is not generally replaced by a pronoun when it follows a preposition. For example, in answer to the question "Is the book on the table?" one does not say "Yes, the book is on it." Rather, one repeats the noun: "Yes, the book is on the table."

You (formal singular)—You only have to establish that this pronoun is an object of a preposition.

> *For whom is the book? It's for* **you.**
>
> > Function: object of preposition *for*
> > Selection: **usted**

> ¿Para quién es este libro? Es para **usted.**

Them—Always plural. In Spanish a noun referring to a thing is not replaced by a pronoun when it follows a preposition. For example, in answer to the question "Do you live near the mountains?" one does not say, "Yes, I live near them." Instead, one repeats the noun or shortens the answer: **"Sí, vivo cerca de las montañas"** or **"Sí, vivo cerca"** ("Yes I live near the mountains" or "Yes, I live near"). If the antecedent of *them* is a person, you will need to determine the gender of the antecedent.

Are you leaving with the girls? Yes, I'm leaving with them.

1. Function: object of preposition *with*
2. Antecedent: **Las chicas** (*girls*) is feminine.
3. Selection: **ellas**

¿Sales con las chicas? Sí, salgo con **ellas**.

object of preposition **con**

Are you going with the children? No, I'm going without them.

1. Function: object of preposition *without*
2. Antecedent: **Los niños** (*children*) is masculine.
3. Selection: **ellos**

¿Vas con los niños? No, voy sin **ellos**.

object of preposition **sin**

Once again we remind you that the types of objects must be identified within the Spanish sentence. Watch the following pitfalls.

1. Object of a preposition in English ⟶ Direct object in Spanish

Are you looking at the flowers? Yes, I am looking at *them.*

    Function in English: object of preposition *at*
       You are looking at what? At them.
    Function in Spanish: direct object pronoun
       The Spanish verb **mirar** means *to look at.*
       The word *at* is contained within the verb; mirar
       is not followed by a preposition. Since there is no
       preposition, the object is direct.

¿Miras las flores? Sí, **las** miro.
               |
          direct object pronoun

Are you looking for the book? Yes, I am looking for it.

    Function in English: object of the preposition *for*
       You are looking for what? For it.
    Function in Spanish: direct object pronoun
       The verb **buscar** means *to look for.* The
       word *for* is contained within the verb; buscar
       is not followed by a preposition. Since there is no
       preposition, the object is direct.

¿Buscas el libro? Sí, **lo** busco.
              |
      direct object pronoun.

2. Subject in English ⟶ Indirect object in Spanish

With some Spanish verbs (V) the equivalent of a subject pronoun
(S) in English is an indirect object (IO) in Spanish.

I like the car.
| | |
S V DO

Me gusta el coche.
| | |
IO V S

He needs a pencil.
  | | |
  S   V   DO

Le falta un lápiz.
 | | |
IO V   S

Let us go over this transformation step-by-step.

1. Transform the English sentence using an indirect object (IO) in place of the subject (S).

> *I* like the car.   =   The car is pleasing *to me.*
>   "*to me* is pleasing the car"
>   IO   V   S

> *He* needs a pencil. =   A pencil is lacking *to him.*
>   "*to him* is lacking a pencil"
>   IO   V   S

2. Express the transformed sentence in Spanish.

> Me gusta el coche.
> "to me is pleasing the car"

> Le falta un lápiz.
> "to him is lacking a pencil"

Here is a list of some of the common verbs that require an indirect object in Spanish where English uses a subject.

doler	*to hurt*
faltar	*to be lacking, to be missing, to need*
gustar	*to be pleasing, to like*
interesar	*to be interesting*
parecer	*to seem*
quedar	*to remain*

SUMMARY

Below is a flow chart of the steps you have to follow to find the Spanish equivalent of each English object pronoun. It is important that you do the steps in sequence, because each step depends on the previous one.

DO = Direct object in the Spanish sentence
IO = Indirect object in the Spanish sentence
OP = Object of a preposition in the Spanish sentence

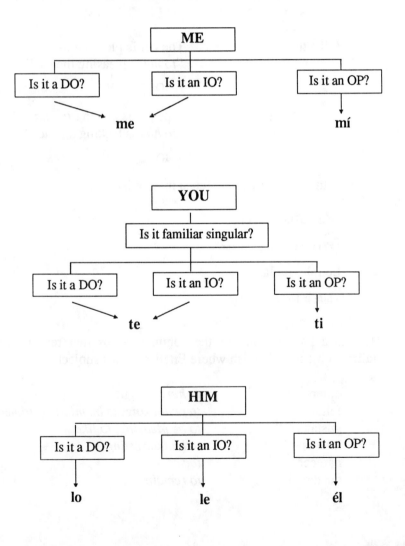

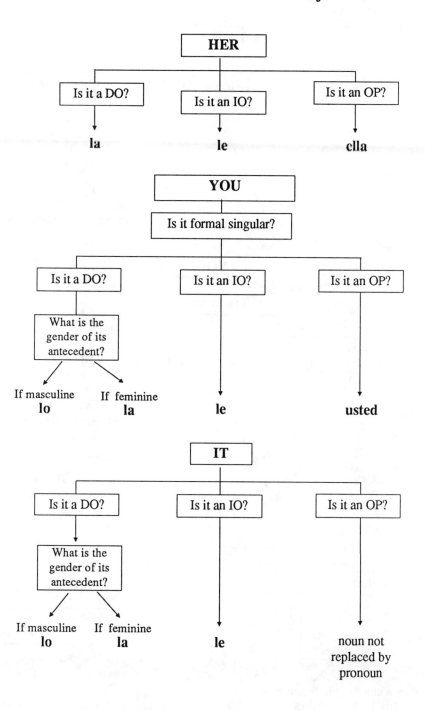

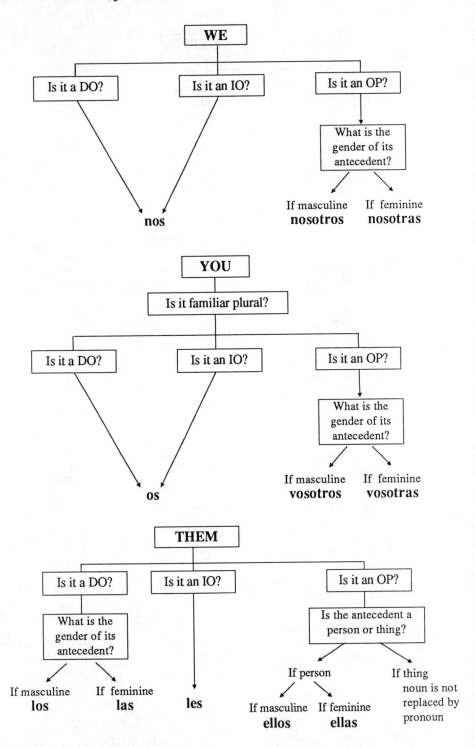

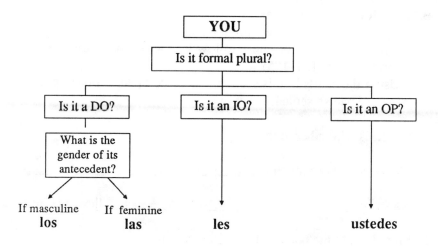

Practice

A. In the following sentences:
- Underline the object pronoun.
- Circle the letters which correspond to its function in the sentence: Direct object (DO), Indirect object (IO), or Object of a preposition (OP).

1. He bought it with the money he had earned.	DO	IO	OP
2. Mary went with him to the movies.	DO	IO	OP
3. She lifted the book and placed the letter under it.	DO	IO	OP
4. The children saw me as I was leaving.	DO	IO	OP
5. The teacher gave us the exam today.	DO	IO	OP
6. The radio was given to you as a present.	DO	IO	OP

B. In the following sentences:
  • Circle the English object pronoun.
  • Fill in the steps you must follow to choose the correct Spanish form (see pp. 184–195).
  • Using the charts in this section, fill in the Spanish object pronoun in the Spanish sentences below.

1. Robert is taking her to the party.

    a. Function of pronoun: _____

    Roberto _____ lleva a la fiesta.

2. Mary bought the book and then she read it.

    a. Function of pronoun: _____

    b. Antecedent: _____

    c. Gender: masculine

    María compró el libro y entonces _____ leyó.

3. The teacher spoke to them about the exam yesterday.

    a. Function of pronoun: _____

    La profesora _____ habló del examen ayer.

4. Did you write Paul? No, but I will write him today.

    a. Function of pronoun: _____

    ¿Le escribiste a Pablo? No, pero _____ escribiré hoy.

5. Is this sandwich for Tom? No, it's for you.

    a. Familiar or formal: Familiar

    b. Function of pronoun: _____

    c. Number of pronoun: _____

    ¿Es este sandwich para Tomás? No, es para _____.

6. Go with her.

    a. Function of pronoun: _____

    Vaya con _____.

What is an Interrogative Pronoun?

An **interrogative pronoun** is a word that replaces a noun and introduces a question. Interrogative comes from *interrogate*, to question.

In English: Different interrogative pronouns are used depending on whether you are referring to a "Person" (this category includes human beings and live animals) or a "Thing" (this category includes objects and ideas). Also the interrogative pronoun referring to persons changes according to its function in the sentence.

A. PERSONS

Who is used for the subject of the sentence.

        Who lives here?
         |
        subject

        Who are they?
         |
        subject

Whom is used for the direct object, indirect object, and the object of a preposition.

> *Whom* do you know here?
> |
> direct object

> To *whom* did you speak?
> |
> indirect object

> From *whom* did you get the book?
> |
> object of preposition *from*

In informal English *who* is often used instead of *whom,* and prepositions are placed at the end of the sentence, separated from the interrogative pronoun to which they are linked.

> *Who* do you know here?
> |
> instead of *whom*

> *Who* did you speak *to*?
> | |
> instead of *whom*   preposition

> *Who* did you get the book *from*?
> | |
> instead of *whom*   preposition

Whose is the possessive form and is used to ask about possession or ownership.

> *Whose* pencil is this?
> |
> possessive

> They are nice cars. *Whose* are they?
> |
>   possessive

B. THINGS

What refers only to things, and the same form is used for subject, direct object, indirect object, and the object of a preposition.

> *What* happened?
> |
> subject

> *What* do you want?
> |
> direct object

> *What* do you cook with?
> |
> object of preposition *with*

C. "WHICH ONE," "WHICH ONES"

Which one, which ones can refer to both persons and things; they are used in questions that request the selection of one (*which one*, singular) or several (*which ones*, plural) from a group. The words *one* and *ones* are often omitted. These interrogative pronouns may be used as a subject, direct object, indirect object, and object of a preposition.

> All the teachers are here. *Which one* teaches Spanish?
> |
> singular subject

> I have two cars. *Which one* do you want to take?
> |
> singular direct object

> There are many children here.
> With *which ones* do you want to speak?
> |
> plural object of the preposition *with*

In Spanish: There are four interrogative pronouns: **quién** (*who*) **qué** (*what*), **cuál** (*which*) and **cuánto** (*how much, how many*).

Let us look at each of the English interrogative pronouns and see how to find the Spanish equivalent.

A. PERSONS

1. *Who, whom* and *whose* = **quién** or **quiénes**
   It agrees in number with the noun it refers to.

   Who—It is a subject pronoun. You will need to determine if the subject asked about is singular or plural.

   Since there is no English equivalent for **quiénes,** both the singular and plural forms translate alike in English. A question with **quién** asks for a singular response:

¿**Quién** viene?	**Juan** viene.
singular subject	singular subject
Who is coming?	*John is coming.*

   A question with **quiénes** asks for a plural response.

¿**Quiénes** vienen?	**Juan, Roberto y Miguel** vienen.
plural subject	plural subject
Who is coming?	*John, Robert and Michael are coming.*

   If you don't know if the response is going to be singular or plural, use the singular form.

   Whom—It is the direct object, indirect object, and object of preposition form. You will need to determine if the object asked about is singular or plural.

¿Con **quién** sales?	Salgo con Roberto.
singular	singular response
With whom are you leaving?	*I'm leaving with Robert.*

¿Con **quiénes** sales?   Salgo con mis amigos.
　　　｜   ｜
　　plural   plural response

*With **whom** are you leaving?*   *I'm leaving with my friends.*

It will often be necessary to restructure English sentences that contain *who* or *whom* separated from the preposition in order to use **quién(-es)** correctly in Spanish.

The following sentences have been restructured to avoid the dangling preposition (see p. 169).

Who are you writing to? ⟶
　｜　　　　　　　　　｜
subject form of   preposition
interrogative

To whom are you writing?
　　　｜
object form of interrogative

¿**A quién** le escribes?

Who are you leaving with? ⟶
　｜　　　　　　　　｜
subject form of   preposition
interrogative

With whom are you leaving?
　　　｜
object form of interrogative

¿**Con quién** sales?

Who did you buy the gift for? ⟶

subject form of   preposition
interrogative

For whom did you buy the gift?

object form of interrogative

¿**Para quién** compraste el regalo?

Whose—It is the possessive interrogative. You will need to restructure English sentences using *whose* in order to use the correct word order in Spanish. To restructure replace *whose* with "of whom" and invert the word order of the subject and verb.

Whose car is it?

"of whom is the car"

¿**De quién** es el coche?

B. THINGS

What = **qué**
It has only one form since it is invariable.

What are you studying this semester?
¿**Qué** estudias este semestre?

What is that?
¿**Qué** es esto?

NOTE: **Qué** can also be used as an interrogative adjective (see p. 148). As an interrogative adjective **qué** is followed by a noun and means *what* or *which*.

¿**Qué** libro tienes?
Which book do you have?

C. "WHICH ONE," "WHICH ONES"

Which one or *which ones* = **cuál** or **cuáles**
There are two forms to agree in number with the noun replaced depending on whether you want to say *which one* (singular) or *which ones* (plural).

> **Which one** *do you need?*
> ¿**Cuál** necesitas?

> **Which ones** *do you need?*
> ¿**Cuáles** necesitas?

If the English word *one/ones* is not expressed, use the verb to determine whether to use **cuál** or **cuáles**. If the verb is singular, use cuál; if the verb is plural, use **cuáles**.

> **Which** *of the girls is Spanish?*
> ¿**Cuál** de las chicas es española?
>   singular   singular verb

> **Which** *of the girls are Spanish?*
> ¿**Cuáles** de las chicas son españolas?
>   plural   plural verb

QUÉ vs. CUÁL (which is. . .?, which are. . .?)

• ¿**qué + ser**. . .? is used when the expected answer is a definition.

> **What is** *the Nobel Prize?*

> The expected answer is a definition
> of the Nobel Prize. Therefore, ¿**qué**
> **es?** is used for *What is*. . .?

¿Qué es el Premio Nobel?

What are the Panamerican Games?

> The expected answer is a definition of
> the Panamerican Games. Therefore,
> ¿qué son? is used for *What are. . .?*

¿Qué son los Juegos Panamericanos?

• ¿cuál (-es) + ser. . .? is used when the expected answer provides one
of a number of choices and answers the question *which one(-s)* of
many.

What is your favorite novel?

> The expected answer will explain which
> novel of the many that exist is the favorite.
> Therefore, ¿cuál es? is used for *What is. . .?*

¿Cuál es su novela favorita?

What are the countries of Europe?

> The expected answer will explain which countries
> of the many in the world are European. Therefore,
> ¿cuáles son? is used for *What are. . .?*

¿Cuáles son los países de Europa?

NOTE: If the "what?" of the English question means *which one*
or *which ones*, then use cuál(-es).

There is another interrogative pronoun that we will now examine
separately since it does not follow the same pattern as the ones
above.

D. "HOW MUCH," "HOW MANY" = cuánto (-a), cuántos(-as)

This interrogative pronoun has four forms that change according to
the gender and number of the antecedent, that is, the noun replaced
by the pronoun.

	SINGULAR	PLURAL
MASCULINE	cuánto	cuántos
FEMININE	cuánta	cuántas

To determine the proper form follow these steps:

1. Determine the antecedent.
2. Determine the gender of the antecedent.
3. Determine the number of the antecedent.

> *I have a lot of paper. **How much** do you want?*
>
>   1. Antecedent: **El papel** (*paper*)
>   2. Gender: masculine
>   3. Number: singular
>   4. Selection: **cuánto**

Tengo mucho papel. ¿**Cuánto** quieres?

> *I have a lot of soup. **How much** do you want?*
>
>   1. Antecedent: **la sopa** (*soup*)
>   2. Gender: feminine
>   3. Number: singular
>   4. Selection: **cuánta**

Tengo mucha sopa. ¿**Cuánta** quieres?

> *I have a lot of books. **How many** do you want?*
>
>   1. Antecedent: **los libros** (*books*)
>   2. Gender: masculine
>   3. Number: plural
>   4. Selection: **cuántos**

Tengo muchos libros. ¿**Cuántos** quieres?

I have a lot of magazines. ***How many*** *do you want?*

1. Antecedent: **las revistas** (*magazines*)
2. Gender: feminine
3. Number: plural
4. Selection: **cuántas**

Tengo muchas revistas. ¿**Cuántas** quieres?

Practice

A. The following sentences contain interrogative words.
- Circle the interrogative pronoun.
- Determine its function: Subject , Object, or Possessive .
- Restructure the sentence if necessary.
- Fill in the Spanish equivalent of the interrogative.

1. Whose sweater is this?

   Function: _____

   Restructure the sentence: _____

   ¿ _____ es este suéter?

2. Who are you talking to?

   Function: _____

   Restructure sentence: _____

   ¿A _____ le hablas?

3. Who is coming to see you? My friends.

   Function: _____

   Number of pronoun: _____

   ¿ _____ vienen a verte? Mis amigos.

B. Circle the correct Spanish equivalent of *What is*? or *what are*?

1. What is your favorite movie?   ¿Qué es?   ¿Cuál es?

2. What are killer bees?   ¿Qué son?   ¿Cuáles son?

3. What are the largest cities
   in Latin America?   ¿Qué son?   ¿Cuáles son?

4. What is Tegucigalpa?   ¿Qué es?   ¿Cuál es?

5. What is the capital of Peru?   ¿Qué es?   ¿Cuál es?

C. The following are sentences with "how much" or "how many."
   • Fill in the steps you have to follow to choose the correct Spanish
     equivalent.
   • Then fill in the Spanish interrogative in the Spanish sentences
     below.

1. Here are the pencils. How many do you need?

   a. Antecedent: _____

   b. Gender: Masculine.

   c. Number: _____

   Aquí tienes los lápices. ¿ _____ necesitas?

2. I just made this salad. How much do you want?

   a. Antecedent: _____

   b. Gender: Feminine

   c. Number: _____

   Acabo de preparer esta ensalada. ¿ _____ quieres?

3. I'll bring the napkins for the party. How many should I buy?

   a. Antecedent: _____

   b. Gender: Feminine

   c. Number: _____

   Voy a traer las servilletas a la fiesta. ¿ _____
   debo comprar?

What is a Demonstrative Pronoun?

A **demonstrative pronoun** is a word that replaces a noun previously mentioned, **the antecedent**, as if pointing to it. Demonstrative comes from *demonstrate*, to show.

In English: The singular demonstrative pronouns are *this (one)* and *that (one)*; the plural forms are *these* and *those*.

Here are two suitcases. *This one* is big and *that one* is small.

The books are on the shelves. *These* are in Spanish, *those* in English.

As with the demonstrative adjectives, *this (one), these* refer to a person or an object near the speaker; *that (one), those* to a person or an object away from the speaker.

In Spanish: Demonstrative pronouns are the same words as the demonstrative adjectives except that all pronoun forms carry a written accent mark in order to distinguish the pronouns from the adjectives. (See **What is a Demonstrative Adjective?**, p. 151.)

TO POINT OUT	SINGULAR		PLURAL	
	MASCULINE	FEMININE	MASCULINE	FEMININE
ITEMS NEAR THE SPEAKER	éste	ésta	éstos	éstas
ITEMS NEAR THE PERSON SPOKEN TO	ése	ésa	ésos	ésas
ITEMS AWAY FROM THE SPEAKER AND PERSON SPOKEN TO	aquél	aquélla	aquéllos	aquéllas

As pronouns, these words replace the demonstrative adjective + noun; they agree in number and gender with the noun replaced.

To choose the correct form, follow these steps.

1. Determine the antecedent.
2. Determine the gender and number of the antecedent.
3. Determine the relationship of the antecedent to the speaker or person spoken to.
4. Based on Steps 1 and 2 choose the correct form from the chart.

Look at the following examples.

> *Give me the magazine;* ***this one.***

> 1. Antecedent: **la revista** (*magazine*)
> 2. Gender and number: feminine singular
> 3. Relationship: near the speaker
> 4. Selection: **ésta**

Déme la revista; **ésta.**

Give me the books; these (ones).

      1. Antecedent: **los libros** (*books*)
      2. Gender and number: masculine plural
      3. Relationship: near the speaker
      4. Selection: **éstos**

Déme los libros; **éstos.**

Give me the pencil near you; that one.

      1. Antecedent: **el lápiz** (*pencil*)
      2. Gender and number: masculine singular
      3. Relationship: near the person spoken to
      4. Selection: **ése**

Déme el lápiz; **ése.**

Give me the notebooks over there; those (ones).

      1. Antecedent: **los cuadernos** (*notebooks*)
      2. Gender and number: masculine plural
      3. Relationship: away from the speaker and person spoken to
      4. Selection: **ésos**

Déme los cuadernos; **ésos.**

NEUTER DEMONSTRATIVE PRONOUNS

Spanish also has three demonstrative pronouns that are used to refer to an idea, item, or previous statement which has no gender or whose gender is not known. These pronouns are therefore said to be neuter in gender and are invariable, that is, they do not change form.

      esto   *this (one)*
      eso   *that (one)*
      aquello   *that (one)*

What is this?

> Since it isn't known what "this" is, its gender is also
> unknown. Therefore, the neuter form **esto** is used.

¿Qué es **esto?**

That's not true.

> *That* refers to a previous statement which has no
> gender. Therefore, the neuter form **eso** is used.

Eso no es verdad.

What is that over there?

> Since it isn't known what "that" is, its gender is also
> unknown and the neuter form **aquello** is used.

¿Qué es **aquello?**

"THE ONE," "THE ONES"

There is another demonstrative pronoun which we will now examine
separately because it does not follow the same pattern as the ones above.

In English: The demonstrative pronouns *the one* and *the ones,* unlike
this one and *that one,* do not point out a specific object, but instead
introduce a clause that helps us identify an object by giving additional information about it. There is a singular form *the one* and a
plural form *the ones.* They are often followed by the relative
pronoun *that* or *which* (see **What is a Relative Pronoun?**, p. 227).

> What book are you reading?
> I am reading *the one (that)* I bought yesterday.

> Clause: *the one that I bought yesterday* gives us
>   additional information about *the book.* Notice that
>   the relative pronoun *that* can be omitted in English.
> Number: *The one* is singular.

Which houses do you prefer?
I prefer *the ones that* are on Columbus Street.

> Clause: *the ones that are on Columbus Street* gives us
> additional information about *the houses*.
> Number: *The ones* is plural.

In Spanish: Forms of the definite article **el, la, los, las** are used as the equivalent of the English demonstrative *the one(s)*. The definite article agrees in number and gender with the noun replaced. *The one* or *the ones* can be used (1) to introduce a clause and (2) to show possession.

1. The definite article + **que** is used to introduce a clause.

The relative pronoun *that* (**que**) is often omitted in English. However, the relative pronoun *that* must be expressed in Spanish. (See **What is a Relative Pronoun?**, p. 227.)

To choose the correct form of *the one(s)* follow these steps.

1. Find the antecedent.
2. Determine the gender and number of the antecedent.
3. Select the proper form of the definite article + **que**.

Look at the following examples.

> *What book are you reading?* **The one (that) I bought yesterday.**
>
> > Antecedent: **el libro** (*book*) is masculine singular.

> ¿Qué libro lees? **El que** compré ayer.
>
> masc. sing.

Which houses do you prefer? The ones (that) are on Columbus St.

> Antecedent: **las casas** (*house*) is feminine plural.

¿Qué casas prefieres? **Las que** están en la Calle Colón.

<u>   </u>

fem. pl.

2. The definite article + **de** is used to show possession.

> *Whose house are you living in? My father's.*

Just as "my father's house" can only be expressed in Spanish by the structure "the house of my father" a similar Spanish structure must be used to say "my father's." In this case the word-for-word English translation of the Spanish structure is "the one of my father." In Spanish "the one" agrees in gender and number with its antecedent, here "the house."

To choose the correct form, follow these steps.

1. Restructure the possessive phrase.
2. Find the antecedent of *the one* or *the ones*.
3. Determine the gender and number of the antecedent.
4. Select the proper form of the definite article + **de**.

Let us apply the rules to the following examples.

> *Which house are you selling? My father's.*

> 1. Restructure: My father's = the one of my father
> 2. Antecedent: house
> 3. Gender and number: **La casa** (*house*) is feminine singular.
> 4. Selection: **la de**

¿Qué casa vendes? **La de** mi padre.

<u>   </u>

fem. sing.

*Which books are you reading? **The teacher's.***

   1. Restructure: The teacher's = the ones of the teacher
   2. Antecedent: books
   3. Gender and number: **Los libros** (*books*) is masculine plural.
   4. Selection: **los de**

¿Qué libros lees? **Los del** professor.

masc. pl.

Practice

A. In the following sentences:
   - Circle the demonstrative pronouns.
   - Fill in the steps you would follow to choose the correct Spanish form.
   - Using the chart in this section fill in the Spanish demonstrative pronoun in the Spanish sentences below.

1. She did not buy my house but she did buy this one.

   a. Antecedent: _____

   b. Relationship: _____

   c. Gender and number: feminine _____

   Ella no compró mi casa pero sí compró _____ .

2. Which notebook is yours? That one?

   a. Antecedent: _____

   b. Relationship: _____

   c. Gender and number: masculine _____

   ¿Qué cuaderno es tuyo? ¿ _____ ?

3. That really bothers me.

a. Antecedent: _____ .

b. Relationship: _____

c. Gender and number: _____

_____ me molesta mucho.

4. The new houses are more expensive than those over there.

a. Antecedent: _____

b. Relationship: _____

c. Gender and number: feminine _____

Las casas nuevas son más caras que _____ .

5. What is this?

a. Antecedent: _____

b. Relationship: _____

c. Gender and number: _____

¿Qué es _____ ?

B. The following sentences contain the expression "the one" or "the ones" in the Spanish equivalent.
   • Fill in the steps you would follow to choose the correct Spanish form.
   • Fill in the correct Spanish equivalent of "the one(s)."

1. Which bookstore do you go to? The one which is near the dorm.

   a. Antecedent: _____

   b. Gender and number: feminine _____

   c. Selection: _____

   ¿A qué librería vas? _____ está cerca de la residencia.

2. What records are you listening to? My brother's.

   a. Restructure: _____

   b. Antecedent: _____

   c. Gender and number: masculine _____

   d. Selection: _____

   ¿Qué discos escuchas? _____ mi hermano.

3. Which glasses are you buying? The ones we saw yesterday.

   a. Antecedent: _____

   b. Gender and number: feminine _____

   c. Selection: _____

   ¿Qué gafas compras? _____ vimos ayer.

What is a Possessive Pronoun?

A **possessive pronoun** is a word that replaces a noun and indicates the possessor of that noun. Possessive comes from *possess*, to own.

> Whose house is that? It's *mine*.

Mine is a pronoun that replaces the words *my house* and shows who possesses the house.

In English: Here is a list of the possessive pronouns.

SINGULAR		
1st PERSON	mine	
2nd PERSON	yours	
3rd PERSON	his hers its	
PLURAL		
1st PERSON	ours	
2nd PERSON	yours	
3rd PERSON	theirs	

Possessive pronouns never change their form, regardless of the thing possessed; they refer primarily to the possessor.

> Is that your house? Yes, it's *mine*.
> Are those your keys? Yes, they're *mine*.

The same possessive pronoun (*mine*) is used, although the objects possessed are different in number (*house* is singular, *keys* is plural).

> John's car is blue. *His* is blue.
> Mary's car is blue. *Hers* is blue.

Although the object possessed is the same (*car*), the possessive pronoun is different because the possessor is different (*John* is masculine singular; *Mary* is feminine singular).

In Spanish: The possessive pronouns have the same forms as the stressed possessive adjectives. (See **What is a Possessive Adjective?**, p. 138.) Like English, Spanish possessive pronouns refer to the possessor but unlike English, they must agree in number and gender with the person or object possessed. In addition, the possessive pronoun is preceded by the definite article which also agrees in gender and number with the noun possessed. So there are masculine and feminine forms in both the singular and plural.

The first letters of the possessive pronoun refer to the possessor and the ending of the possessive pronoun agrees with the noun possessed.

*Where are your books? **Mine** are in the living room.*

Possessor: *Mine* 1st pers. sing. = **mí-**
Possessed: **Los libros** (*books*) is masc. pl. = **los** + **-os**

mascl. pl. endings

¿Dónde están tus libros? **Los míos** están en la sala.

1st pers. sing.
possessor

Here are the steps you should follow in choosing the correct possessive pronoun.

1. Indicate the possessor. This is shown by the first letters of the possessive pronoun

mine	**mí-**
yours	**tuy-**
his, hers, yours	**suy-**
ours	**nuestr-**
yours	**vuestr-**
theirs, yours	**suy-**

2. Find the noun possessed and determine its gender and number. Choose the definite article + the possessive pronoun ending according to the gender and number of that noun.

- If the noun possessed is masculine singular, use the definite article **el** and add **-o** to the first letters of the possessor.

    ¿Dónde está el libro?   **El mío** está sobre la mesa.
                 |
          noun possessed
          masc. sing.

    Where is the book?   ***Mine*** *is on the table.*

- If the noun possessed is feminine singular, use the definite article **la** and add **-a** to the first letters of the possessor.

    ¿Dónde está la revista?   **La mía** está sobre la mesa.
                 |
          noun possessed
          fem. sing.

    Where is the magazine?   ***Mine*** *is on the table.*

- If the noun possessed is masculine plural, use the definite article **los** and add **-os** to the first letters of the possessor.

    ¿Dónde están los libros? **Los míos** están sobre la mesa.
                 |
          noun possessed
          masc. pl.

    Where are the books?   ***Mine*** *are on the table.*

- If the noun possessed is feminine plural, use the definite article **las** and add **-as** to the first letters of the possessor.

¿Dónde están las revistas? **Las mías** están sobre la mesa.

noun possessed
fem. pl.

Where are the magazines? *Mine are on the table.*

3. Select the proper form according to the two steps listed above.

Let us apply the steps to the following examples.

She is reading her magazines. He is reading yours.

1. Possessor: **tuy-**
2. Noun possessed: **Las revistas** (*magazines*) is feminine plural.
3. Selection: **las + -as**

Ella lee sus revistas. El lee **las tuyas.**

Susana forgot her notebook but we have ours.

1. Possessor: **nuestr-**
2. Noun possessed: **El cuaderno** (*notebook*) is masculine singular.
3. Selection: **el + -o**

Susana olvidó su cuaderno pero tenemos **el nuestro.**

NOTE: The definite article is not used when the possessive pronoun follows a form of the verb **ser** (*to be*).

¿Es este tu abrigo?
No, no es **mío. El mío** es más grande.

possessive pronoun   article + possessive
without article   pronoun
after **ser**

Is this your coat?
*No, it's not **mine.**   **Mine** is larger.*

Practice

In the following sentences:
- Circle the possessive pronoun.
- Fill in the steps you would follow to choose the correct Spanish form.
- Using charts in this section, fill in the proper Spanish possessive pronoun in the Spanish sentences below.

1. I won't take your car. I'll take mine.

   a. Possessor: _____

   b. Noun possessed: _____

   c. Gender and number: masculine _____

   d. Article and ending: _____

   No tomaré tu coche. Tomaré _____.

2. I'm not going with my parents. I'm going with hers.

   a. Possessor: _____

   b. Noun possessed: _____

   c. Gender and number: masculine _____

   d. Article and ending: _____

   No voy con mis padres. Voy con _____.

3. I'm not going with my parents. I'm going with his.

    a. Possessor: _____

    b. Noun possessed: _____

    c. Gender and number: masculine _____

    d. Article and ending: _____

No voy con mis padres. Voy con _____.

4. This isn't your (fam. sing.) suitcase. Yours is bigger.

    a. Possessor: _____

    b. Noun possessed: _____

    c. Gender and number: feminine _____

    d. Article and ending: _____

No es su maleta. _____ es más grande.

5. Paul's racquet is broken; he'll use ours.

    a. Possessor: _____

    b. Noun possessed: _____

    c. Gender and number: feminine _____

    d. Article and ending: _____

La raqueta de Pablo está rota. Va a usar _____.

What is a Relative Pronoun?

A **relative pronoun** is a word that serves two purposes:

1. As a pronoun it stands for a noun or another pronoun previously mentioned. The noun or pronoun referred to is called the **antecedent**.

This is the boy who broke the window.
|
antecedent

2. It introduces a **subordinate clause,** that is, a group of words having a subject and verb separate from the subject and verb of the main sentence. A subordinate clause cannot stand alone as a complete sentence.

main clause   subordinate clause

This is the boy who broke the window.

subject verb

Who broke the window is not a complete sentence.

The above subordinate clause is also called a **relative clause** because it starts with a relative pronoun *who*. The relative clause gives us additional information about the antecedent *boy*.

In English: The selection of most relative pronouns depends on the function of the relative pronoun in the relative clause, and on whether the antecedent is a "Person" (this category includes human beings and live animals) or a "Thing" (this category includes objects and ideas). Sometimes, two different relative pronouns can be used to say the same thing. Here are the most common English relative pronouns.

A. SUBJECT OF THE RELATIVE CLAUSE

Refers to a person: *who*

> She is the only student *who* answered all the time.
> |
> antecedent
> *Who* is the subject of *answered*.

Refers to a thing: *which*

> The movie *which* is so popular was in Spanish.
> |
> antecedent
> *Which* is the subject of *is*.

Refers to a person or a thing: *that*

> She is the only student *that* answered all the time.
> |
> antecedent
> *That* is the subject of *answered*.

> This is the book *that* is so popular.
> |
> antecedent
> *That* is the subject of *is*.

As you can see, you sometimes have the choice between two relative pronouns; *who* and *that*, for instance.

B. DIRECT OBJECT OF THE RELATIVE CLAUSE

Although the direct object relative pronouns are often omitted in English, we have indicated them in parentheses because they must be expressed in Spanish.

Refers to a person: *whom*

> This is the student (*whom*) I saw yesterday.
> |
> antecedent
> *Whom* is the direct object of *saw*.
> (*I* is the subject of the relative clause.)

Refers to a thing: *which*

> This is the book (*which*) Paul bought.
> |
>   antecedent

> *Which* is the direct object of *bought*.
> (*Paul* is the subject of the relative clause.)

Refers to a person or a thing: *that*

> This is the student (*that*) I saw yesterday.
> |
>   antecedent

> *That* is the direct object of *saw*.
> (*I* is the subject of the relative clause.)

> This is the book (*that*) Paul bought.
> |
>   antecedent

> *That* is the direct object of *bought*.
> (*Paul* is the subject of the relative clause.)

C. INDIRECT OBJECT OR OBJECT OF PREPOSITION IN THE RELATIVE CLAUSE

Refers to a person: *whom*

> Here is the student I was speaking *to*.
> |
>   antecedent

This English structure cannot be translated word-for-word into Spanish for two reasons: (1) The Spanish language does not permit dangling prepositions (see p. 169), and (2) the relative pronoun omitted in English must be expressed in Spanish. To establish the Spanish structure, you must restructure the English sentence, placing the preposition within the sentence and adding a relative pronoun. If you are not sure where to place the preposition and the relative pronoun, remember that they follow immediately after the antecedent.

SPOKEN ENGLISH ——————→ RESTRUCTURED
Here is the student   Here is the student *to*
I was speaking *to*.   *whom* I was speaking.

Whom is the indirect object of *was speaking*.

Here is the stud|ent I was talking *about*.
     antecedent

As in the case of the indirect object, spoken English often omits the relative pronoun and places the preposition at the end of the sentence. Again, you will have to restructure the sentence.

SPOKEN ENGLISH ——————→ RESTRUCTURED
Here is the student I   Here is the student *about*
was speaking *about*.   *whom* I was speaking.

Whom is the object of the preposition *about*.

Refers to a thing: *which*

Here is the mus|eum he gave a painting *to*.
     antecedent

SPOKEN ENGLISH ——————→ RESTRUCTURED
Here is the museum he   Here is the museum *to*
gave the painting *to*.   *which* he gave the painting.

Which is the indirect object of *gave*.

D. POSSESSIVE MODIFIER "WHOSE"

The possessive modifier *whose* is a relative pronoun which does not change form regardless of its function or antecedent.

Find the wom|an *whose* car was stolen.
     antecedent

Whose is a possessive modifying *car*.

Look at the house *whose* roof burned.

|

antecedent

Whose is a possessive modifying *roof.*

USE OF RELATIVE PRONOUNS

Relative clauses are very common. We use them in our everyday speech without giving much thought to why and how we construct them. The relative pronoun allows us to combine in a single sentence two thoughts which have a common element.

Let us look at a few examples to see how we construct relative clauses:

- Sentence A: The students passed the exam.
  Sentence B: They studied.

1. Identify the element the two sentences have in common.

   The students and *they;* both words refer to the same persons. *The students* is the antecedent. *They* will be replaced by a relative pronoun.

2. Establish the function of the relative pronoun in the relative clause. It will have the same function as the word it replaces.

   The relative pronoun will be the subject of *studied.* (*They* is the subject of *studied.*)

3. Choose the relative pronoun according to whether its antecedent is a person or a thing.

   They refers to *students.* Therefore, its antecedent is a person.

4. Select the relative pronoun.

Who or *that* is the subject relative pronoun referring to a person.

5. Place the relative pronoun after its antecedent.

The students *who* studied passed the exam.

or

The students *that* studied passed the exam.

antecedent   relative clause

- Sentence A: The Spanish teacher is nice.
  Sentence B: I met her today.

  1. Common element: *the Spanish teacher* and *her*
  2. Function of *her:* direct object
  3. Antecedent: *The Spanish teacher* is a person.
  4. Selection: *whom* or *that*
  5. Placement: *whom* or *that* after *the Spanish teacher*

  The Spanish teacher, *whom* I met today, is nice.

  antecedent   relative clause

In spoken English, you would say: "The Spanish teacher I met today is nice." Notice that the relative pronoun *whom* is left out, making it difficult to identify the two clauses.

- Sentence A: Mary read the book.
  Sentence B: I was speaking about it.

  1. Common element: *book* and *it*
  2. Function of *it:* object of the preposition *about*
  3. Antecedent: *The book* is a thing.
  4. Selection: *which*
  5. Placement: *about which* after *the book*

Mary read the book *about which* I was speaking.

         antecedent   relative clause

In spoken English, you would say: "Mary read the book I was speaking about." Notice that the preposition is at the end and that there is no relative pronoun.

In Spanish: Relative pronouns are used just as they are in English. The main difference is that, unlike English where the relative pronoun can sometimes be omitted at the beginning of a relative clause, the relative pronoun must always be expressed in a Spanish sentence.

There are four main relative pronouns in Spanish: **que, cual, quien,** and **cuyo.** Each has its own rules for use and position.

A. SUBJECT AND OBJECT OF RELATIVE CLAUSE

Que in conversational (spoken and written) Spanish
Cual in formal (spoken and written) Spanish

Both forms correspond to *that, which,* and *who* as relative pronoun subjects and *that, which* and *whom* as relative pronoun objects.

1. **Que** is invariable; it does not change form.

    *Here is the phone **that (which)** isn't working.*

       antecedent   relative pronoun
          thing   subject

Aquí está el teléfono **que** no funciona.

    *John is the student **that (who)** answered.*

       antecedent   relative pronoun
         person   subject

Juan es el estudiante **que** respondió.

*Joe is the boy **that (whom)** I admire most.*

antecedent   relative pronoun
person   object

José es el chico **que** yo admiro más.

This is the book I bought.

Add the relative pronoun that has been omitted because
it will have to be expressed in the Spanish sentence.

*This is the book **that** (or **which**) I bought.*

antecedent   relative pronoun
thing   object

Este es el libro **que** compré.

2. **Cual** has four forms in order to agree with its antecedents in gender and number: **el cual, la cual, los cuales, las cuales.** Since it changes forms to agree with its antecedent it can often express more clearly the antecedent it is replacing.

*John is the student **that** answered.*
Juan es el estudiante **que** respondió.

conversational Spanish

Juan es el estudiante **el cual** respondió.

formal Spanish

*Mary is the student **that** answered.*
María es la estudiante **que** respondió.

conversational Spanish

María es la estudiante **la cual** respondió.

formal Spanish

B. OBJECT OF A PREPOSITION IN RELATIVE CLAUSE

- if the antecedent is a person
preposition + **quien** = singular antecendent
preposition + **quienes** = plural antecedent

You will often need to restructure the English sentence before attempting to put it into Spanish.

John is the boy I'm going with.
|
antecedent
singular

You must restructure the dangling preposition.

*John is the boy with **whom** I am going.*
Juan es el chico con **quien** salgo.

The girls I'm writing to live in Madrid.
|
antecedent
plural

You must restructure the dangling preposition.

*The girls to **whom** I am writing live in Madrid.*
Las chicas a **quienes** les escribo viven en Madrid.

This is the boy I was talking about.
|
antecedent
singular

You must restructure the dangling preposition.

*This is the boy about **whom** I was talking.*
Este es el chico de **quien** hablaba.

- if the antecedent is a thing
preposition + **que** in conversational Spanish

> *This is the book I was talking about.*
> |
>   antecedent
>
> You must restructure the dangling preposition.

> *This is the book about **which** I was talking.*
> Este es el libro de **que** hablaba.

B. **Cuyo**, a relative adjective corresponds to *whose*. Although it is not a pronoun, but an adjective, we have included it here because it introduces a relative clause. **Cuyo** has four forms: **cuyo, cuya, cuyos, cuyas**. The endings agree with the item or person possessed which will follow the word **cuyo**.

> *The lady **whose** son is sick is our neighbor.*
> | |
> possessor   item possessed
>   person
>
> The relative possessive will agree with **el hijo**
> (*son*) which is masculine singular.

> La mujer **cuyo** hijo está enfermo es nuestra vecina.
>   └─┬─┘
>   masc. sing.

> *The man **whose** house you bought is Mr. Gómez.*
> | |
> possessor   item possessed
>   thing
>
> The relative possessive will agree with
> **la casa** (*house*) which is feminine singular.

> El hombre **cuya** casa compraste es el señor Gómez.
>   └─┬─┘
>   fem. sing.

The following chart provides a summary of the relative pronouns.

ENGLISH	SPANISH

A. SUBJECT
    PERSON: who/what
    THING: that/which
	A. SUBJECT
	    PERSON: **que**
	    THING: **que**

B. DIRECT OBJECT
    PERSON whom/that
    THING: that/which
	B. DIRECT OBJECT
	    PERSON OR THING:
	    CONVERSATIONAL: **que**
	    FORMAL: **cual**

C. OBJECT OF A PREPOSITION
    PERSON: whom
    THING: which
	C. OBJECT OF A PRESPOSITION
	    PERSON: preposition + **quien(es)**
	    THING: preposition + **que**

D. POSSESSIVE: whose	D. POSSESSIVE: **cuyo**

Let's review the steps for selecting the correct relative pronoun.

1. Find the relative clause; restructure the English clause if necessary.
2. Find the relative pronoun.
3. Find the antecedent.
4. Determine the function of the relative pronoun in Spanish.

    Is it a subject or object? If yes, use
        A. **que** in conversational Spanish
        B. **cual** in formal Spanish
    Is it the object of a preposition? If yes, use
        A. preposition + **que** if the antecedent is a thing
        B. preposition + **quien(es)** if the antecedent is a person
    Is it a possessive? If yes, use
        forms of **cuyo** + the item possessed. **Cuyo** will not agree with the antecedent; it agrees with the item possessed.

5. Select the pronoun according to the antecedent (except for **cuyo**).

Let's apply these steps to the following examples.

> *The lady **who** is my neighbor is from Ecuador.*

>> 1. Relative clause: who is my neighbor
>> 2. Relative pronoun: who
>> 3. Antecedent: the lady (**la señora**)
>> 4. Function of *who:* subject
>> 5. Selection: **que**

La señora **que** es mi vecina es de Ecuador.

> *Peter and Joe are the boys I was talking to.*

>> 1. Relative clause: I was talking to
>>   Restructure: *to whom I was talking*
>> 2. Relative pronoun: whom
>> 3. Antecedent: Peter and Joe
>> 4. Function of *whom:* object of preposition *to*
>> 5. Selection: **quienes**

Pedro y José son los chicos a **quienes** hablaba.

> *Mary is the girl **whose** father is from Greece.*

>> 1. Relative clause: whose father is from Greece
>> 2. Relative pronoun: whose
>> 3. Antecedent: girl
>> 4. Function of *whose:* possessive
>>   Item possessed: father (**el padre**)
>> 5. Selection: **cuyo padre**

María es la chica **cuyo** padre es de Grecia.

RELATIVE PRONOUNS WITHOUT ANTECEDENTS

There are relative pronouns that do not refer to a specific noun or pronoun. Instead they refer to an antecedent which has not been expressed or to a whole idea.

In English: There are two relative pronouns that may be used without an antecedent.

What meaning *that which.*

> Here is *what* I read.
> |
> no antecedent

> I don't know *what* happened.
> |
> no antecedent

>> It is easy to see that there is no antecedent, because antecedents (nouns and pronouns) come just before relative pronouns.

Which referring back to a whole idea, not to a specific noun or pronoun.

> You speak many languages, *which* is an asset.
> |
>> Antecedent of *which:* the fact that you speak many languages

> She didn't do well, *which* is too bad.
> |
>> Antecedent of *which:* the fact that she didn't do well

In Spanish: The expression **lo que** is the equivalent of the English *what* or *which* without antecedent. **Lo que** is used in conversational Spanish and refers to an idea or previously mentioned statement or concept which has no gender. It can function as a subject or object.

> *What bothers me most is the heat.*
> |
>> Relative pronoun referring to an idea; it is used as a subject.

> **Lo que** me molesta más es el calor.

What you are saying isn't true.
|

Relative pronoun referring to a previous
statement; it is used as an object.

Lo que dices no es verdad.

I didn't hear what he said.
|

Relative pronoun referring to a previous
statement; it is used as an object.

No oí **lo que** dijo.

Do you know what my daughter did?
|

Relative pronoun referring to an idea; it
is used as an object.

¿Sabes **lo que** hizo mi hija?

Practice

A. In the following sentences:
  • Underline the relative pronoun.
  • Circle the antecedent.
  • Identify the function of the relative pronoun by circling the appropriate identification: Subject (s), Direct object (DO), Indirect object (IO), Object of a preposition (OP), or Possessive (P).

1. I received the letter that you sent me.   S   DO   IO   OP   P

2. That is the woman who speaks Spanish.   S   DO   IO   OP   P

3. Here comes the man to whom I lent money.   S   DO   IO   OP   P

4. This is the book whose title I had forgotten.   S   DO   IO   OP   P

5. Paul is the student about whom I spoke.   S   DO   IO   OP   P

B. Using a relative pronoun, combine the series of two sentences below into one sentence.
   • Fill in the blanks showing the steps you have to follow.
   • On the line below, write the combined sentence.

1. The girl is nice. She lives next door.

   a. Common elements: _____ / _____

   _____ is the antecedent.

   _____ will be replaced by a relative pronoun.

   b. Function of relative pronoun: _____

   c. Type of antecedent: _____

   d. Selection: _____

   _____

   _____

2. He spoke on a new topic. I knew nothing about it.

   a. Common elements: _____ / _____

   _____ is the antecedent.

   _____ will be replaced by a relative pronoun.

   b. Function of relative pronoun: _____

   c. Type of antecedent: _____

   d. Selection: _____

   _____

   _____

3. The new student is Mexican. You are talking about her.

    a. Common elements: _____ / _____

    _____ is the antecedent.

    _____ will be replaced by a relative pronoun.

    b. Function of relative pronoun: _____

    c. Type of antecedent: _____

    d. Selection: _____

    _____

    _____

C. Find the Spanish equivalent of the English relative pronoun in the following sentences.
- Circle the relative pronoun.
- Fill in the blanks for each step you have to follow.
- Then, fill in the appropriate Spanish relative pronoun in the Spanish sentence.

1. The house that I am buying is very modern.

    a. Relative clause: _____

    b. Function of relative pronoun: _____

    c. Antecedent: _____

La casa _____ compro es muy moderna.

2. The student who is sleeping works at night.

    a. Relative clause: _____

    b. Function of relative pronoun: _____

    c. Antecedent: _____

El estudiante _____ duerme trabaja por la noche.

3. This is the article I was talking about.

    a. Relative clause: _____

      Restructured: _____

    b. Function of relative pronoun: _____

    c. Antecedent: _____

Este es el artículo de _____ hablaba.

4. What he said was a lie.

    a. Relative clause: _____

    b. Function of relative pronoun: _____

    c. Antecedent: _____

_____ dijo fue una mentira.

5. Susan is the girl whose father is the engineer.

    a. Relative clause: _____

    b. Function of relative pronoun: _____

c. Antecedent: _____

d. Gender and number of noun possessed: el padre =

_____

Susana es la chica _____ padre es el ingeniero.

What are Indefinites and Negatives?

Indefinites are words that refer to persons, things, or periods of time that are not specific or that are not clearly defined.

In English: Some common indefinites are *someone, anybody, something, some day*. These indefinite words are often paired with negative words which are opposite in meaning: *no one, nobody, nothing,* and *never.*

INDEFINITES	NEGATIVES
someone / anyone	no one
somebody / anybody	no body
something / anything	nothing
some day / any day	never

In conversation indefinites frequently appear in questions while negatives appear in answers.

> Q: Is *anyone* coming tonight?
> A: *No one.*

Q: Do you have *anything* for me?
A: *Nothing.*

Q: Are you going to Europe *some day?*
A: *Never.*

English sentences can be made negative in one of two ways (see
What are Affirmative and Negative Sentences?, p. 60):

- with the word *not*

    I am studying.
    I am *not* studying.

- with a negative word

    No one is coming.
    He has *never* seen a movie.

English allows only one negative word (either *not* or any of the
other negative words) in a sentence (or clause). When a sentence
contains the word *not*, another negative word cannot be used in that
same sentence.

"I am *not* studying *nothing.*"
|
negative word

This sentence contains a double
negative: *not* and *nothing.*
It is incorrect English.

When a sentence contains the word *not*, the indefinite word that is
the opposite of the negative word must be used.

I am *not* studying *anything.*
|
indefinite word

Let us look at another example.

I have *nothing.*
|
negative word

Nothing is the one negative word.

I do *not* have *anything.*
|
indefinite word

This sentence contains *not;* therefore, the
word *anything* is substituted for *nothing.*

"I do *not* have *nothing.*"

This sentence contains a double negative: *not*
and *nothing.* It is incorrect English.

In Spanish: As in English, the indefinite and negative words exist as
pairs of opposites. A few of the most common indefinites and
negatives are listed in the chart.

INDEFINITES		NEGATIVES	
something	algo	*nothing*	nada
some, any	algún, alguno	*none*	ningún, ninguno
someone *somebody*	alguien	*no one* *nobody*	nadie
some day *always* *sometimes*	algún día siempre a veces	*never*	nunca
also, too	también	*not . . . either*	tampoco
either, or	o	*neither . . . nor*	ni

Notice that most indefinites begin with the letters **alg-** and the negatives begin with **n-.**

Contrary to English a negative word (not an indefinite) is used in a Spanish sentence that contains *no* meaning *not*. An indefinite word cannot appear in a negative Spanish sentence.

ENGLISH: I do *not* have *anything*.
                                  | |
                                not   indefinite word

SPANISH: **No** tengo **nada.**
                                  | |
                                not   negative word (*nothing*)

The following formula for indefinite and negatives in English and Spanish will help you use them correctly.

ENGLISH: ***not*** + indefinite word
SPANISH: **no** + negative word

In order to use the indefinites and negatives correctly in Spanish it will often be necessary to reword the English sentence so that it is a word-for-word translation of the Spanish sentence.

*I do **not** see **anybody.***
        | |
      not   +   indefinite

Word-for-word: "I do *not* see *nobody*"
                                  |
                              negative

No veo a **nadie.**
  | |
 no   +   negative

Follow these steps to find the Spanish equivalent of an English sentence with *not* + an indefinite word:

1. Locate the indefinite word in the English sentence.
2. From the chart choose the negative word that is the opposite of the English indefinite word.
3. Restructure the English sentence using *not* + the negative word chosen under 2 above.
4. Put the sentence into Spanish.

Let us apply the steps outlined above to the following sentences.

*I do not want to eat **anything**.*

      1. Indefinite: anything
      2. Negative: nothing
      3. Restructure: "I do *not* want to eat *nothing*"

No quiero comer **nada.**

*I don't (do not) know **anyone** here.*

      1. Indefinite: anyone
      2. Negative: no one
      3. Restructure: "I *don't* know *no one* here"

No conozco a **nadie** aquí.

Practice

In the following sentences:
- Locate the indefinite word or phrase.
- Determine what is the negative word that is the opposite of the English indefinite word.
- Restructure the English sentence using *not* + the negative word chosen above.
- Fill in the negative phrase in the Spanish sentence.

1. I'm not going to do that ever.

    a. Indefinite: _____

    b. Negative: _____

    c. Restructure: _____

  No voy a hacer eso _____.

2. John isn't going to the party either.

    a. Indefinite: _____

    b. Negative: _____

    c. Restructure: _____

  Juan no va a la fiesta _____.

3. We don't have anything to do.

    a. Indefinite: _____

    b. Negative: _____

    c. Restructure: _____

  No tenemos _____ que hacer.

4. They don't know anyone in Bogotá.

    a. Indefinite: _____

    b. Negative: _____

    c. Restructure: _____

  No conocen a _____ en Bogotá.

Answer Key

What is a Noun? 1. student, classroom, teacher 2. Wilsons, tour, Mexico 3. honesty, policy 4. Lisa, carpet, bedroom 5. figure skating, event, Winter Olympics 6. scientists, elephants 7. allegiance, flag, United States, America 8. Buenos Aires, capital, Argentina, city 9. truth, fiction 10. Monday, day, week 11. manager, intelligence, sense, humor

What is Meant by Gender? A. 1. masculine 2. ? 3. feminine 4. masculine 5. ? 6. ? 7. feminine 8. ? B. 1. masculine 2. feminine 3. feminine 4. masculine 5. masculine 6. masculine 7. feminine 8. masculine

What is Meant by Number? A. 1. P 2. S 3. P 4. P 5. S 6. S B. 1. S 2. ES 3. S 4. ES 5. S 6. ES

What are Articles? 1. D 2. I 3. I 4. D 5. D 6. I   B. 1. los libros 2. la mesa 3. las clases 4. el teléfono 5. los coches 6. la hermana C. 1. unos 2. una 3. unas 4. un 5. unos 6. una

What is the Possessive? 1. the parents of some children 2. the office of the doctor 3. the life of a dog 4. the soccer coach of the girls 5. the mother of Gloria Smith

What is a Verb? 1. purchase 2. were 3. enjoyed, preferred 4. ate, finished, went 5. realized, dreamt 6. felt, seems 7. stayed, expected 8. was, to see, struggle, to get 9. attended, to celebrate 10. increases, remains

What is an Infinitive? A. 1. swim 2. be 3. go 4. have 5. do 6. write B. 1. to do 2. study 3. to learn 4. sing 5. to travel

What are Auxiliary Verbs? Words in *italics* should be underlined once; words in **bold** should be underlined twice A. 1. *is* **talking** 2. *did* **finish** 3. *have* **seen** 4. *would* **buy** *do* **have** 5. *does* **live** 6. *were* **doing**   B. 1. will 2. — *are* is a Spanish auxiliary and is expressed with **estar** 3. did 4. — *had* is a Spanish auxiliary and is expressed with **haber** 5. do

What is a Subject?   1. Q: What rang? A: The bell. Q: Who ran out? A: The children.   2. Q: Who took the order? A: One waiter. Q: Who brought the food? A: Another.   3. Q: Who voted? A: The first-year students (or The students).   4. Q: What assumes? A: That. Q: Who is right? A: I.   Q: Who says? A: They.   Q: What is a beautiful language? A: Spanish.

What is a Pronoun?   *The antecedent is between parentheses.* 1. she (Mary), him (Peter) 2. they (coat, dress) 3. herself (Mary) 4. we (Paul, I) 5. it (bed)

What is a Subject Pronoun?   A. 1. they / *ellos* or *ellas* 2. you / *tú* 3. I / *yo* 4. you / *vosotros* or *vosotras.* 5. we / *nosotros* or *nosotras.* 6. he, she, it / *él, ella, usted*   B. 1. *yo* 2. O 3. *nosotros* or *nosotras* 4. O 5. *ellos* 6. *ellas*

What is Meant by Familiar and Formal You?   1. ustedes / ustedes 2. tú / tú 3. usted / usted 4. vosotros / ustedes 5. tú / tú 6. usted / usted

What is a Verb Conjugation?   A. STEM: com- ENDINGS: -o, -es, -e, -emos, -éis, -en BEBER: bebo, bebes, bebe, bebemos, bebéis, beben B. STEM: escrib- ENDINGS: -o, -es, -e, -imos, -ís, -en VIVIR: vivo, vives, vive, vivimos, vivís, viven

What ar Affirmative and Negative Sentences?   A. 1. We do not (don't) want to leave class early. 2. He did not (didn't) do his homework yesterday. 3. Teresa will not (won't) go to Chile this summer. 4. Robert cannot (can't) go to the restaurant with us. 5. Mr. Smith does not (doesn't) play tennis every day.   B. 1. do no 2. did not 3. will not 4. cannot 5. does not   C. 1. do 2. did 3. 0 4. 0 4. does 5. does

What are Declarative and Interrogative Sentences?   A. 1. Did Richard and Kathy study all evening? 2. Does your brother eat a lot? 3. Do the girl's parents speak Spanish?   B. 1. did 2. does 3. do C. 1. did 2. does 3. do   D. 1. Richard and Kathy 2. your brother 3. the girl's parents

What are Some Equivalents of *To Be*?   A. 1. CHAR ser 2. COND
estar 3. COND estar 4. CHAR ser 5. COND estar 6. COND estar 7. CHAR
ser   B. 1. ser 2. estar 3. estar 4. ser 5. estar 6. ser 7. ser 8. ser
C. 1. hay 2. estar 3. hay 4. estar 5. hay

What is Meant by Tense?   1. time 2. simple 3. two 4. auxiliary
5. main 6. & 7. present and past 8. simple 9. future or conditional
10. simple

What is the Present Tense?   A. 1. reads 2. is reading 3. does read
B. 2. lee 3. lee

What is the Past Tense?   A. (*The answers to 1 and 2 can be in any
order.*) 1. imperfect 2. preterite 3. simple 4. preterite 5. imperfect
B. 1. was, played = imperfect 2. did do = preterite 3. came home =
preterite; was watching = imperfect 4. used to go = imperfect 5. had,
broke = preterite 6. traveled = imperfect

What is a Participle?   A. 1. -ing 2. present 3. past 4. past
5. present 6. past   B. 1. PRES 2. PAST 3. INF 4. PAST 5. PRES

What is a Progressive Tense?   A. 1. PRES 2. PRES PROG
3. PRES PROG 4. PRES 5. PRES

What is Meant by Mood?   A. 1. verbs 2. indicative 3. present
4. past 5. future 6. imperative 7. subjunctive   B. 1. IND 2. SUBJ
3. SUBJ 4. IND 5. SUBJ 6. IND

What is the Subjunctive?   1. SUBJ 2. SUBJ 3. IND 4. SUBJ 5. SUBJ
6. SUBJ 7. IND

What is the Imperative?   A. 1. Study every evening. 2. Let's go to
the movies once a week.   B. 1. Don't sleep in class. 2. Don't talk a
lot.   C. 1. C 2. C 3. P 4. C 5. C 6. P

What are the Perfect Tenses?   A. 1. to have 2. past particple (of the main verb) 3. four 4. four 5. two 6. auxiliary verb   B. 1. had gone—past perfect 2. has left—present perfect 3. will have graduated—future perfect 4. would have studied—conditional perfect; had remembered—past perfect 5. have seen—present perfect

What is the Future?   A. 1. will study, study 2. 'll clean, clean 3. shall leave, leave 4. won't (will not) finish, finish 5. will be, be B. 1. I wonder, be 2. is probably, be 3. might have, have 4. must have, have 5. is probably going to win, win

What is the Conditional?   1. conditional 2. conditional, imperfect subjunctive 3. conditional or imperfect subjunctive 4. present, future 5. conditional 6. pluperfect subjunctive, conditional perfect 7. imperfect

What is a Reflexive Verb?   A. 1. themselves 2. herself 3. yourself 4. yourselves 5. themselves   B. 1. se 2. nos 3. te 4. se 5. me 6. se

What is Meant by Active and Passive Voice?   A. 1. cow, cow A 2. bill, Bob's parents, P 3. bank, bank A 4. everyone, everyone A 5. spring break, all P   B. 1. are taking, P, The final exam is being taken by all the students. 2. brought, PP, The children were brought to the park by the teacher. 3. will read, F, That article will be read by people all over the world.

What is an Adjective?   1. noun 2. pronoun 3. descriptive 4. possessive 5. interrogative 6. demonstrative 7. number 8. gender

What is a Descriptive Adjective?   A. *The noun or pronoun described is between parentheses.* 1. young (man), Spanish (newspaper) 2. pretty (she), red (dress) 3. interesting (it) 4. old (piano), good (music) 5. tired (Paul), long (walk)   B. 1. a jacket of leather 2. my notebook of history 3. shoes of tennis 4. cake of chocolate 5. juice of tomato 6. a house of brick

What is a Possessive Adjective? A. 1. possessor, *mi, tu, su, su,* number, singular, plural, -s 2. possessor, *nuestr-, vuestr-,* number and gender, *-o, -a, -os, -as* B. 1. a. her b. 3rd pers. sing. c. singular, *su* 2. a. our b. 1st pers. pl. c. fem. sing., *nuestra* 3. a. your b. 2nd pers. sing. c. plural, *tus* 4. a. their b. 3rd pers. pl. c. singular, *su* 5. a. his b. 3rd pers. sing. c. singular, *su*

What is an Interrogative Adjective? A. *The noun modified is between parentheses.* 1. how much (time) 2. which (book) 3. what (exercises) 4. how many (sisters) 5. which (house) B. *The English interrogative adjectives are between parentheses.* 1. (how many) shirts, *cuántas* 2. (how much) wine, *cuánto* 3. (how many) telephones, *cuántos* 4. (how much) salad, *cuánta*

What is a Demonstrative Adjective? A. *The noun modified is between parentheses.* 1. that (restaurant) 2. these (jeans) 3. those (houses) 4. this (magazine) B. *The demonstrative adjective circled is between parentheses.* 1. (that) a. near the person spoken to b. ese d. singular, *ese* 2. (this) a. near the speaker b. este d. singular, *esta* 3. (those) a. away from the speaker and person spoken to b. aquel c. plural, *aquellas*

What is Meant by Comparison of Adjectives? A. The teacher is older than the students. 2. He is less intelligent than I am. 3. Mary is as tall as Paul. 4. That boy is the worst in the school 5. Paul is a better student than Tom. B. 1. composition 2. exercises 3. girl 4. student

What is an Adverb? *The word modified is between parentheses.* 1. early (arrived) 2. really (quickly), quickly (learned) 3. too (tired) 4. reasonably (secure) 5. very (well), well (speaks)

What is a Conjunction? The words to be circled are in **bold**; the words to be underlined are in *italics*. 1. *Mary* **and** *Paul* were going to study *French* **or** *Spanish.* 2. *She did not study* **because** *she was too tired.* 3. *Not only had he forgotten his ticket,* **but** *he had forgotten his passport as well.* 4. *She knew he was mean,* **yet** *she still loved him.* 5. *They borrowed money* **so** *they could go to France.*

What is a Preposition?   A. 1. about 2. from, by 3. around 4. contrary to 5. between   B. 1. In whose car are you riding? 2. I got the scholarship for which I applied. 3. To which movie is John going? 4. Richard is the boy about whom I was talking?

What are Objects?   1. Q: The children took what? A: A shower. DO 2. Q: They ate what? A: The meal. DO Q: They ate with what? A: Pleasure. OP 3. Q: He sent what? A: A present. DO   Q: He sent a present to whom? A: His brother. IO 4. Q: They paid for what? A: The books. OP   Q: They paid with what? A: A credit card. OP

What is an Object Pronoun?   A. 1. it, DO 2. him, OP 3. it, OP 4. me, DO 5. us, IO 6. you IO   B. 1. her a. direct object, *la* 2. it a. direct object b. the book, *lo* 3. them a. indirect object, *les* 4 . him a. indirect object, *le* 5. you b. object of a preposition c. sing., *ti* 6. her a. object of a preposition, *ella*

What is an Interrogative Pronoun?   A. 1. whose, P, Of whom is the sweater?, *De quién* 2. who, O, To whom are you talking?, *quién* 3. who, S, plural, *Quiénes*   B. 1. ¿Cuál es? 2. ¿Qué son? 3. ¿Cuáles son? 4. ¿Qué es? 5. ¿Cuál es? .   C. 1. a. pencils, c. plural, *Cuántos* 2. a. salad c. singular, *Cuánta* 3. a. napkins c. plural, *Cuántas*

What is a Demonstrative Pronoun?   A. 1. this one a. house b. near the speaker c. singular, *ésta* 2. that one a. notebook b. near the person spoken to c. singular, *ése* 3. that a. unknown b. near the person spoken to c. neuter / sing., *Eso* 4. those (over there) a. houses b. away from the speaker and person spoken to c. plural, *aquéllas* 5. this a. unknown b. near the speaker c. neuter / singular, *esto*   B. 1. a. bookstore b. singular c. *la, la que* 2. a. the ones of my brother b. records c. plural d. *los, los de* 3. a. glasses b. plural c. *las, las que*

What is a Possessive Pronoun?   1. a. mine = *mí*- b. car c. singular d. el -o, *el mío* 2. a. hers = *suy*- b. parents c. plural d. los -os, *los suyos* 3. a. his = *suy*- b. parents c. plural d. los -os, *los suyos* 4. a. yours = *tuy*- b. suitcase c. singular d. la -a, *la tuya* 5. a. ours, nuestr- b. racquet c. singular d. la -a, *la nuestra*

What is a Relative Pronoun?   A. *The antecedent is between parentheses.* 1. that (letter) DO 2. who (woman), S 3. whom (man), IO 4. whose (book), P 5. whom (student), OP   B. 1. girl / she; girl; she; subject, person; who or that; The girl who (that) lives next door is nice. 2. topic / it; topic; it; object of a preposition; thing; which; He spoke on a new top about which I knew nothing. 3. student / her; student; her; object of a preposition; person; whom; The new student about whom you are talking is Mexican.   C. *The relative pronoun is between parentheses.* 1. (that) a. that I am buying, direct object c. house, thing, *que* 2. (who) a. who is sleeping b. subject c. student, person, *que* 3. (relative pronoun is not expressed) a. I was talking about / about which I was talking b. object of a preposition c. article, thing, *que* 4. (what) a. what he said b. subject c. non-existent, *lo que* 5. (whose) a. whose father is the engineer b. possessive c. girl d. masc. sing. *cuyo*

What are Indefinites and Negatives?   1. a. ever b. never c. I'm not going to do that never. *nunca* 2. a. either b. neither c. John isn't going to the party neither. *tampoco* 3. a. anything b. nothing c. we don't have nothing to do, *nada* 4. a. anyone b. no one c. they don't know no one in Bogotá, *nadie*

Index

264